THE
DANNY FORD
YEARS AT
CLEMSON

THE
DANNY FORD
YEARS AT
CLEMSON

ROMPING AND STOMPING

LARRY WILLIAMS

Charleston · London

THE
History
PRESS

Published by The History Press
Charleston, SC 29403
www.historypress.net

Copyright © 2012 by Larry Williams
All rights reserved

Cover images appear courtesy of the Clemson University Sports Information Department.

First published 2012

Manufactured in the United States

ISBN 978.1.60949.705.7

Library of Congress CIP data applied for.

CONTENTS

ACKNOWLEDGEMENTS

The first question many people asked upon hearing that I was writing a book on Danny Ford's time at Clemson was: "You mean no one has written a book on that yet?"

The answer, remarkably, is no. But there's actually a good explanation for it. Ford, you see, is not interested in writing a book. He's not interested in anyone writing one of those "as told to" deals in which he spends hours upon hours rehashing things he's not comfortable rehashing and then someone transcribes it all and puts it together for a book.

There are some things better left unsaid, some wounds that don't need reopening with a tell-all memoir. That's the impression I got from him a few years ago when I asked if he'd ever be interested in such a project, and almost before I finished the question, he responded with an unequivocal "No."

Given that, Ford is probably the first person I need to thank for being so understanding with this undertaking. Initially, the idea was to write a lengthy series on his Clemson tenure for my employer, Tigerillustrated. com. The success of that endeavor inspired the idea for a deeper exploration that's present in these pages.

Ford neither endorsed nor forbade either work. Aside from a 2011 interview with him conducted by my boss, Cris Ard, every quote from Ford in this book is taken from assorted media accounts of his tenure as it was unfolding.

There are probably some details that Ford and possibly others would prefer to have not been unearthed. But the intent was to provide a definitive, unvarnished account of his days at Clemson—the good, the bad and the ugly. The intent was also to be accurate and fair to Ford and everyone else in the book. I sincerely hope those aspirations were reached.

Thank you to Clemson sports information director Tim Bourret for his typical above-and-beyond helpfulness. Every photograph in this book was provided by his office, and that made the process so much easier. He also allowed me to rummage through all of his old Ford files, plus stacks of archived *Orange and White* issues and other news accounts. And, of course, he relayed some of the many memorable anecdotes and one-liners that made Ford such a fascinating figure.

Thank you to some of Ford's former players, including Vance Hammond, Joe Bostic, Steve Kenney and Levon Kirkland. The thrust of this book was research, giving readers a sense of what it was like as events were unfolding, and thus you don't see many quotes from people reflecting on stuff that happened a long time ago. But conversations with people who played for him, among others, did provide a feel for those times.

Thank you to Clemson men Al Adams, Sanford Rogers, Sam Blackman and Mickey Plyler for sharing their institutional knowledge of the Ford days. Thank you to Kerry Capps, a longtime chronicler of the Tigers, for his encouragement and recollections. Thank you to my boss for always being open to ideas such as this one, and for giving me the time to carry them out.

Thank you to Clemson's Special Collections staffers for their patience and generosity in allowing me to sift through all kinds of documents and clippings and pictures and a bunch of other stuff that helped make this book interesting.

Thank you to Adam Ferrell, Jessica Berzon and the staff of The History Press for having total trust in the vision for this work and the implementation of it.

And finally, thank you to my beautiful wife and two daughters for their eternal patience and understanding every time I disappeared to work on this fascinating project.

INTRODUCTION

One of the most enduring snapshots of Danny Ford's coaching tenure at Clemson comes from the first day of his coaching tenure at Clemson.

Ford, an Alabama boy all of thirty years old, took over a shattered fan base after Charley Pell's abrupt departure to Florida. He was so nervous at his introductory press conference that he drew the ire of Tiger legend Frank Howard.

Howard watched the proceedings from the back of the room. He was a believer in Ford, but the Tigers' new coach was so uncomfortably nervous and meek on the podium that Howard yanked him aside afterward and told him he couldn't hear him.

"You've got to romp and stomp," Howard told him that day.

It's hard to fathom Ford ever being at a loss for words or noticeably uncomfortable in front of a room full of people. But he most certainly was on that day. Eventually, though, Ford learned to just be himself. And he did plenty of romping and stomping, putting his own endearing, enduring stamp on the Clemson program.

You've probably heard some of the stories and anecdotes that made Ford such an entertaining subject when he was leading Clemson in his own colorful, tobacco-chewing way from late 1978 until his polarizing divorce with the school after the 1989 season.

Maybe you've heard about the time he angrily confronted North Carolina State University's Monte Kiffin at midfield, accusing Kiffin of ratting out Clemson to the NCAA:

"Ain't no telling what I said after the game," Ford told reporters. "But if I said it, I said it."

Maybe you've heard about the time he invented a word:

"Some people call it chemistry, but I don't like that word. We just don't have all our working parts together. We're not clicking. We don't have *clickness.*"

Or maybe you heard about the time after Clemson's 1989 annihilation of Florida State, when a Seminoles fan masquerading as a reporter asked him how he was going to like probation:

"(Expletive) you, buddy."

So many stories and anecdotes, so many details worth exploring even twenty-two years after Ford cleaned out his office at the Jervey Athletic Center.

The man lives the simple life on a farm a few miles from campus and is more beloved than ever in large part because he's so embraceable. Whether he's tailgating with fans before a football game or eating lunch at a greasy spoon or occupying a stool at a dingy downtown bar, Ford doesn't seem too impressed with himself. He walks around as if he's just an average dude, and that tends to resonate with a blue-collar fan base that's still waiting for the program to reclaim the dominating ways last achieved under his watch.

Reporters who didn't have a chance to cover him on a daily basis wish they'd have come along a little earlier. Ford was in South Florida in January 2012 for Clemson's Orange Bowl appearance, and a few days before the game, he meandered into a hotel media hospitality room.

Ford, who was to be inducted into the bowl's Hall of Fame, could've sought out far more regal company. When someone asked him what in the world he was doing hanging around with a bunch of sportswriters on this occasion, Ford responded:

"I'm just looking for a wing and a beer."

He proceeded to hold court with the wide-eyed scribes, Budweiser in hand.

The national title, all those ACC trophies and all those bowl butt-whippings of national powers have a way of minimizing the memories of the heavy price paid for much of the achievement. But he thumbed his nose at the ACC and everyone else that didn't like seeing little 'ole Clemson win big, and that's another reason that he's eternally revered, despite some of the darker moments of his tenure.

Maybe the biggest personal tragedy of Ford's time at Clemson was that he was never able to enjoy his greatest successes for long. Seemed there was always a menacing black cloud hovering close to most of Ford's days in the sun. That's what made the sequence of his forced departure, coming just a few weeks after his program looked like maybe the best in college football during a Gator Bowl thrashing of Major Harris and West Virginia, a haunting but perfect microcosm of his tenure.

The roaring fame achieved under Ford, and the NCAA-imposed infamy that came with it, created a nasty tug of war between athletics and academics. The former won when university president Bill Atchley was forced out in 1985. The latter won in 1990 when Ford, to the outrage of many, suddenly became a full-time farmer. He landed at Arkansas a few years later and compiled a 26-30-1 record in five seasons before returning to the 170-acre farm outside of Clemson in the late 1990s.

The fallout from Ford's parting with Clemson was so powerful that, when the football program was going twenty long and agonizing years without an ACC championship, many fans blamed lack of administrative commitment to football and said the head honchos weren't interested in gridiron greatness. Ford is embraced by plenty of people at Clemson, but still not enough people for his name to grace the prestigious Ring of Honor at Memorial Stadium.

So many things have been written and said about Ford and his tumultuous tenure at Clemson, but so many more of the details and anecdotes have been shrouded by the passage of time—or perhaps clouded by revisionist memories or eliminated altogether by mental blocks. Most people who were around back then remember only bits and pieces, producing gaps and holes that invite a much closer inspection for those attempting to observe a complete picture.

This book, the product of almost two months of intensive research, is an effort to paint such a picture. There's no anniversary to commemorate, no news angle that makes it topical. Bottom line: Ford's time at Clemson is just so darned interesting and captivating, all these years later.

Chapter 1

THE BEGINNING

A mere wall separated Charley Pell's postgame press conference from the high-decibel jubilation of Clemson's locker room beneath the west end zone stands of Memorial Stadium.

The assembled scribes and talking heads had trouble hearing the coach as he gave his thoughts on a 41-23 smashing of rival South Carolina. On multiple occasions, he was interrupted by the joyful eruptions of his players and coaches next door.

"There's a volume you can't turn down," Pell told the reporters.

The volume outside the stadium was equally amplified as fans returned to their tailgates toasting the accomplishments of Pell and the Tigers. The magic of 1977 had given way to dominance in 1978, and Clemson was on top of the world with a ten-win season, an ACC title secured a week earlier with a victory at Maryland and a trip to the Gator Bowl.

Pell took over a team that had won a total of five games under Red Parker in 1975 and 1976. And now he was looking back on an 18-4-1 record in his first two years. It was a giddy, gleeful time for Clemson fans who had endured years of mediocrity and worse before this good fortune.

"This will go down in history as one of the greatest Clemson seasons ever," Pell said in that press conference. "Today was a great victory. It concludes one of the most rewarding seasons I've ever been associated with. Twenty-five great seniors going out with a convincing victory over a good South Carolina team."

Clemson faithful were partying like it was 1959, which happened to be the last time they'd tasted such success. Pell, the Alabama boy who'd taught these Clemson boys how to win, was beloved.

A chronicling of this unrestrained ecstasy is necessary to achieve a proper understanding of the unrestrained grief that was right around the corner. Less than a week later, a report out of Orlando said Pell was interested in the head-coaching vacancy at Florida. Kerry Capps, Clemson beat writer for the *Greenville News*, contacted Pell, and the coach told him the report was "a damn lie."

A day later, Pell acknowledged he was planning on talking with Florida. The Gators had parted ways with Doug Dickey, and Arkansas coach Lou Holtz was the front-runner before changing his mind and deciding to remain with the Razorbacks.

By the morning of Monday, December 4, Pell was interviewing with Florida president Robert Marston at Greenville-Spartanburg Airport. The night before, Pell had assured Tigers athletics director Bill McLellan that he was staying at Clemson. Before noon on Monday, Pell told McLellan he was gone.

McLellan and other school administrators were stunned and tried to convince Pell to stay. He told them his decision was "irrevocable." Players said Pell told them he believed he could not win a national championship at Clemson. He said the move to Florida was a no-brainer because the state sent two hundred high school players to major colleges every year. Some of his players believed he aspired to eventually return to Alabama and coach his alma mater, and this move pushed him closer to that goal.

With signing day in early December, there was an urge on Clemson's part to identify Pell's replacement as soon as possible. A young offensive line coach named Danny Ford, then thirty years of age, was in Charlotte at Shrine Bowl practices when he and other Tigers assistants were summoned back to Clemson so Pell could deliver the news.

Ford's name and face were not instantly recognizable to Clemson fans, mainly because he'd been at Clemson for just two seasons after Pell hired him away from Virginia Tech. But Pell thought a lot of this young coach, and Ford was given much of the credit for an offense that was prolific in 1977 and 1978.

Pell told McLellan and other Clemson officials that they needed to hire Ford, and he said he'd be more than happy to take Ford to Florida if they didn't. On Monday evening, Pell had an emotional meeting with his players at Mauldin Hall, the team's dorm. Receiver Jerry Butler stood up and spoke, telling Pell how much he appreciated him and his ushering of the program from obscurity to prominence. The players gave Pell a standing ovation.

By this time, word began to trickle out that Ford would get strong support as Pell's replacement at a Board of Trustees meeting the next morning. Ford told Dan Foster, columnist for the *Greenville News*, that he wanted the job.

"It's what I've been working for ever since I got out of Alabama. I graduated in 1969, and this is what I've been working for ever since. I feel like we can keep a lot of our staff here."

Asked by Foster what he'd do if another assistant got the job, Ford replied: "I don't think I could be working here for somebody else, if you can put that kindly."

Ford was popular among many players, as evidenced by the petition signed by seventy-three of them endorsing his elevation to head coach. A group of about twenty players, with offensive lineman Steve Kenney serving as spokesman, took the petition to the Student Affairs Committee of the Board of Trustees.

Coach Ford has been almost as important as Coach Pell in turning the program around. He is a first-class coach, recruiter and person. But most important, he is a winner. Call Charley Pell, Jimmy Sharpe, Bill Dooley or Bear Bryant. Most important, call the Clemson Tiger football team. We are the group that goes out Monday through Saturday. We are winners now and know what it takes to climb to the top. At this point, it takes Coach Ford.

When university president R.C. Edwards returned from a business trip to Washington on Monday night, he summoned Ford to his home to talk about the job. Shortly after the discussion began, Kenney and fellow offensive lineman Joe Bostic arrived at the president's house to voice their support for Ford. They waited in a separate room as Edwards finished his meeting with Ford, and Ford didn't know that his players were there.

Kenney, who was a senior in 1978, remembers now that there was some talk of Clemson hiring a big-name coach from elsewhere to replace Pell.

> *I was sad that Coach Pell was leaving, because I really liked him a lot. But I remember thinking immediately after hearing he left: "We've got to get Coach Ford this position." Now I look back and realize I was twenty-two years old, and who did I think I was trying to make Coach Ford the head coach? But you're young, and you don't know any better.*
>
> *I felt pretty strongly about the fact that Danny Ford was going to be a great head coach. The thing that's important is a head coach having a certain presence when he walks into a room. Charley Pell had it. Danny Ford had it. You can't fake that. You've either got it or you don't.*

Ford's promotion occurred quickly, perhaps in part as a result of the success that followed Pell's rapid hiring after Parker's firing in 1976. Clemson said no other candidates were considered.

At his introductory press conference, Ford didn't sugarcoat when he talked about the future. The Tigers were going to have to rebuild after losing many of the stars who helped bring all those wins in 1977 and 1978.

"We've got to go to work. We're a day late and a dollar short right now with some prospects. But we've got a chance to have the best recruiting year we've had in a long while if we can get on the road and get busy. … People say there are challenges at a lot of places. There's not a bigger challenge anywhere in the world than there is right here next year, after losing twenty-six seniors."

Ford was not yet the commanding speaker he later became. He was noticeably nervous at his first public appearance as the Tigers' head coach, and Frank Howard pulled him aside afterward and delivered some pointed advice.

"When you get up in front of that audience, you got to straighten up and look 'em straight in the damn face and pronounce them words so they can understand 'em," Howard told Ford. "I couldn't hear you in the back."

Ford told the Tiger legend that he was nervous. Howard: "You got to romp and stomp." Ford: "It's going to take me a day or so, but I'll be all right."

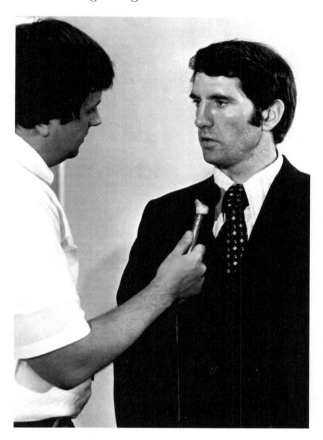

Danny Ford is interviewed
on the day of his hiring as
Clemson's head football
coach. Ford took over
in December 1978 after
Charley Pell abruptly left
for Florida. *Courtesy of
Clemson University Sports
Information Department.*

Pell was planning to stick around and coach the bowl game against Ohio State, but that arrangement didn't last long. Clemson people were angry when they heard stories of Pell getting a head start on his recruiting for the Gators when he was still supposed to be coaching the Tigers. The Associated Press moved a photo of Pell holding up a Gators pennant at a function in Jacksonville, disturbing Tigers supporters even more.

Clemson fans were still in mourning over losing Pell, who told McLellan that Florida was one of the twelve best coaching positions in the country. The knowledge that Pell viewed Clemson as a steppingstone, coupled with the sight of Pell pumping up his new team while still supposedly working for his old one, turned the depression into rage. Bumper stickers that read "Give 'em hell, Pell" were replaced by decals that read "To hell with Pell."

Bostic recalls now that the players didn't want Pell coaching the bowl game.

"It was offensive as hell to think of him coaching us in a bowl game in the state of Florida when he left us for a job in Florida. We didn't want him to get a bunch of positive publicity off our backs. We didn't want recruits in Florida to see us beat Ohio State with him coaching us and then say, 'We need to play for him.'"

Six days after announcing he was leaving for Florida, Pell announced he would not coach the Gator Bowl. He told the media he was hurt by the nastiness directed at him and his family by Clemson supporters, claiming that his eight-year-old son was harassed by other elementary-school students.

Pell took defensive assistants Joe Kines and Dwight Adams to Florida, and Ford faced a monstrous task: get Clemson ready to face Woody Hayes and Ohio State in three weeks. Hayes was sixty-five years old, a head-coaching veteran of thirty-three years who'd amassed a record of 238-71-11.

The entire team was still haunted by the memory of what unfolded at the Gator Bowl the year before. Pittsburgh ripped apart the Tigers in a 34-3 bloodletting that left a smudge on an otherwise special season. Star quarterback Steve Fuller, who threw four interceptions in that defeat, told reporters that Clemson was looking for national respect on this trip to the Sunshine State.

Ford ordered his team to report to Florida a week earlier than the previous year. The team spent a week in Daytona going through unforgiving two-a-days at Mainland High School, even practicing on Christmas Day.

The day before the game, Hayes and Ford were together at a bowl luncheon attended by several hundred people. At Ford's request, Howard was summoned to the podium for some playful verbal sparring with Hayes.

"Something that happened to me might be happening to you pretty soon," Howard told Hayes. "I retired from coaching for health reasons. The alumni was sick of me. Those people at Ohio State damn sure ought to have had enough of you by now.

"Woody, I got a lot of hopes for you in the game tomorrow night. If you kick the sideline markers, I hope you break your toe. If you jump up and take a swing at the goalposts, I hope you break your damn neck."

Ford on the field of the Gator Bowl as his team prepares to play Ohio State in his first game as head coach. Ford later admitted that he was nervous before the game, which the Tigers won 17-15. *Courtesy of Clemson University Sports Information Department.*

The crowd laughed, but Hayes didn't seem amused. During his own speech, he didn't acknowledge Howard's chiding. Hayes had lost five of his previous seven bowl games, including a 35-6 hammering at the hands of Alabama in the 1977 Sugar Bowl.

Ford later said he was so nervous a few hours before the game "that I didn't think I was going to make it." He has told former players he was so apprehensive that he only remembers bits and pieces from the entire night.

Ford experienced some relief when he saw his team put forth an inspired effort that produced a 17-15 victory. End Steve Gibbs blocked an extra point after a second-quarter touchdown, and it ended up being crucial. Jim Stuckey prevented a two-point conversion with a hard hit on quarterback Art Schlichter after a fourth-quarter touchdown.

A final Buckeyes' drive into Clemson territory was foiled when nose guard Charlie Bauman intercepted a Schlichter pass on third-and-5, and that's when the Ford story became a footnote. Hayes slugged Bauman after Bauman was tackled out of bounds on the Buckeyes' sideline.

Most Clemson fans who attended the game didn't realize what had happened. ABC announcers Keith Jackson and Ara Parseghian didn't mention it during the broadcast, and they later claimed they didn't see it happen.

Ford had just returned from a walk on the beach with his wife in the wee hours Saturday morning when he saw reporters waiting for him in the lobby of the team hotel, seeking comments on the Hayes punch.

When ACC commissioner Bob James returned to his hotel room late Friday night after the game, he received a call from Big Ten commissioner Wayne Duke. He apologized to James and assured him that Ohio State's president would impose severe disciplinary action.

Hayes resigned the next morning before leaving Jacksonville. He informed his players of his resignation on the flight back to Columbus.

Ford later received a written apology from Ohio State's administration. The nasty end to Hayes's career didn't keep Ford from beaming about the contributions that fueled his first victory as the Tigers' head man.

"I can't say enough good things about the play of our defense or the coaches who stepped in at a challenging moment and got the job done," Ford told reporters a day after the game. "Because of the coaching change, we were disadvantaged on defense, and there's no other way to say it. Coach Pell was defense-oriented, and the two assistants who went with him to Florida were defensive coaches. Mike Bugar and Mickey Andrews called our defensive signals Friday night, and they did a super job. Our assistant coaches and senior players won the game."

Chapter 2

1979

When the calendar turned to 1979 after an exhilarating Gator Bowl victory over Ohio State, it felt like a new era of Clemson football—and not solely because a young coach named Danny Ford was putting his brand on the program.

Gone were a number of stars who powered the spectacular nineteen-win run in 1977 and 1978. Quarterback Steve Fuller exhausted his eligibility, as did all-everything receiving target Jerry Butler. Both were picked in the first round of the 1979 NFL Draft, Butler going fifth to the Buffalo Bills. Offensive tackle Joe Bostic went in the third round, one of six overall draft picks for the Tigers.

The 17-15 bowl win over the Buckeyes in Ford's first game gave Clemson an 11-1 record and its highest final ranking ever at number six. The personnel losses were so vast that the Tigers were not even ranked heading into 1979.

In an August team meeting, Ford scribbled his team's composition on a chalkboard: twenty seniors, nineteen juniors, thirty-eight sophomores and sixty freshmen. The coach was concerned about depth. He devised a new approach to player use and substitution, announcing a few days before the September 8 opener that no fewer than forty-four players would see the field in the first half against Furman—including as many as twelve players from a highly regarded recruiting class. This tactic was a departure from the methods of Charley Pell, who substituted conservatively.

"This is not an attempt to build for next year or the year after," Ford told reporters at the time. "It's designed to help this year's team. Bear Bryant used this kind of a system to wear his opponents down. We don't have the people to wear anybody down right now, but I'm convinced that it will help us down the road if somebody gets hurt in November or October."

The Tigers still had some key pieces remaining. Bostic's younger brother Jeff anchored the offensive line. Defensive tackle Jim Stuckey, a future first-round draft pick, was back for his senior year. The running back tandem of Lester Brown and Marvin Sims was strong. And there were some young players with promising futures: linebacker Jeff Davis, receiver Perry Tuttle, defensive back Willie Underwood, defensive tackle Steve Durham, defensive back Terry Kinard and others.

Quarterback was a major question mark. The starter entering the season was Billy Lott, a twenty-year-old from Jesup, Georgia. Lott led his high school team to a state title at the age of fourteen and chose Clemson before Fuller blossomed into a star. He ended up sitting the bench in 1977 and 1978, and even with Fuller gone, Lott didn't have a firm hold on the starting job.

This team was led by players who wanted to shape a new identity, players who used the meager preseason predictions as motivation. Ford was apprehensive about replacing so many great players, but a part of him seemed to relish the underdog role.

Ford was far from ecstatic after a 21-0 win over Furman in the opener, saying the Tigers "missed more assignments than any team in the history of football." But he took pride in delivering a shutout, saying that should be the standard for home games at Clemson.

"We don't want to run the score up on anybody, but we don't want anybody to score on us when we're in Death Valley," Ford said in his post-game press conference. "If we're ahead 40-0, we'll put the first team in if they're trying to score. They're not supposed to score in Death Valley."

Clemson then brought the nation's longest active winning streak (eleven games) into a home showdown with Maryland, a team the Tigers beat narrowly late in 1978 to clinch their first ACC title in eleven years. Maryland left Death Valley with a 19-0 victory that brought criticism on Clemson's offense. The Tigers mustered just 195 yards, almost 100 yards less than their worst offensive showing in 1978, and Ford yanked Lott in the middle of the game and replaced him with a freshman named Homer Jordan.

Dan Foster, columnist for the *Greenville News*, was not impressed with what he saw of Clemson in this defeat.

"The Clemson offense is in deep trouble. What they had been afraid they saw the first Saturday, they knew they saw the second."

Ford ended up switching back to Lott the next week as Clemson prepared for a visit from Georgia. Ford said he was going to be patient with a young offense, and he maintained that the Tigers could be a good football team as long as they mixed good defense with a solid kicking game.

Ford did try to simplify the offense in hopes of generating some consistency and confidence. He also wanted to emphasize his desired method of a physical, between-the-tackles running game.

Georgia came in having lost at home to Wake Forest, a defeat Vince Dooley called the most embarrassing loss in his sixteen seasons as the Bulldogs' coach.

Ford, likely in the 1979 season, wearing a tie for one of the few times in his coaching career. *Courtesy of Clemson University Sports Information Department.*

Clemson ended up compounding Dooley's misery, giving him his first 0-2 start by winning 12-7. Sims, the fullback who carried just twice against Maryland, had 145 yards on 25 carries. Backup fullback Tracy Perry had 68 yards on 11 attempts.

The main star of the day was the defense, which kept Georgia out of the end zone until nine seconds remained in the game. The Tigers intercepted three passes and decked the Bulldogs for a safety in the fourth quarter. Ford called it a "big, big win" after the game and said he was going out with his wife to celebrate.

The Tigers had an open date after the Georgia victory, and they returned October 6 with a 17-7 home victory over Virginia. A week later, they went to Virginia Tech and bagged an impressive 21-0 win that was tainted a bit by a rib injury to Brown, the team's leading rusher. Lott was named the ACC's offensive back of the week after rushing for ninety-five yards and throwing for two touchdowns against the Hokies.

By the time Clemson won 28-10 at Duke to push its record to 5-1, the defense-first identity of this team had crystallized. The Tigers were allowing less than seven points a game before that win in Durham, and the defensive players were incensed after the Blue Devils scored a garbage-time touchdown.

The Tigers were in prime position heading into a visit from N.C. State, the team that was picked to win the ACC in the preseason. Maryland had slipped, losing multiple conference games to give Clemson a shot at its second consecutive ACC title. Ford reminded fans that the last five games would be much tougher; the combined record of Clemson's remaining opponents stood at 25-7.

The Tigers found themselves inches short of a big victory over the Wolfpack. Down 16-13 late, Clemson had first-and-goal from the 4 after a 39-yard run by Lott. Three runs by Perry produced 2 yards, and on fourth-and-2 Ford called timeout with 3:17 remaining.

He went for the win, calling for another Perry run off-tackle. As Perry pushed toward the goal line, he thought he was in when he heard a Clemson cheerleader fire the cannon in the end zone. The refs thought otherwise, ruling him down at the 1. Lott was furious at the officials, saying Perry's forward progress carried him into the end zone.

"Maybe I let up just a little when they fired the cannon," Perry told reporters. "I just don't know."

The defense gave the ball back to the offense with 1:40 left, and Clemson took over at the N.C. State 48. The Tigers reached the 30, but Lott was picked off by safety Mike Nall to end it.

Ford, whose team outgained the Wolfpack 356-148 in the 16-13 loss that severely damaged the Tigers' ACC hopes, was questioned by reporters about going for the win. A tie would have given the team a share of the ACC crown.

"We weren't worried about a tie. If you play all day like that and go for a 16-16 tie, it's not worth selling tickets to see. If we had a chance to do it over again, the only thing we'd do differently is not make mistakes."

Stuckey questioned the decision to go for the win. "A tie would have helped us a lot more than a damn loss," he told reporters in the locker room. "We're out of the championship picture now. We've still got a chance at a good record and a bowl. But the ACC title is out."

Wake Forest brought a high-powered offense to Clemson the next week, and the fourteenth-ranked Demon Deacons were regarded as a stiff test. John Mackovic's team had defeated Georgia, Auburn and North Carolina, but it didn't stand a chance against the Tigers' defense. Clemson took over early thanks in part to a thirteen-yard interception return for a touchdown by Jeff Davis, and Wake quarterback Jay Venuto walked away impressed after his team absorbed a 31-0 pounding. He said Davis and Bubba Brown "are the two best linebackers I've ever seen."

"All I saw were orange jerseys all over the field," he told reporters. "They were everywhere."

A few days later, the 6-2 Tigers broke into the UPI coaches' poll at number seventeen. Ford didn't give the distinction much thought. "It's taken us eight weeks to get into the Top Twenty, but it could take us about two hours to blow it," he said at his press luncheon.

Clemson received a rude welcome to Chapel Hill for its next game at North Carolina. The Tigers' police escort to the stadium darted away en route, leaving the team buses to fight traffic on the way to Kenan Stadium. The team arrived much later than scheduled and had to rush through warm-ups.

The Chapel Hill newspaper, in a front-page story, said the invasion of Tiger fans raised the number of rednecks to a level second only to Darlington, South Carolina. The paper later apologized for the barb.

Clemson's defense dominated the Tar Heels' league-leading offense in a 19-10 victory, producing five turnovers. Ford commended the offensive line for taking control of the game in the second half.

With Clemson at number fourteen in both the AP and UPI polls the next week, talk of bowls consumed fans and media. Ford considered it a distraction as his team prepared for a trip to Notre Dame, saying the game "is as big as any bowl game a Clemson team has ever been to."

The Irish had dropped to 6-3 and out of the rankings after a 40-18 loss at Tennessee the previous week. Clemson was ranked second nationally in scoring defense at 7.7 points per game, and the 109-yard rushing average allowed by the Tigers ranked in the Top Ten.

Two years earlier, Notre Dame traveled to Clemson and left with a narrow victory courtesy of some late-game heroics by quarterback Joe Montana. Irish coach Dan Devine didn't enjoy his Death Valley experience, particularly the crowd noise. He refused to shake hands with Tigers coach Charley Pell at midfield. He took some shots at Clemson in the press and said it was "bush" for the 1977 game program to feature the Tigers more prominently than the Irish.

Notre Dame needed a miracle to overcome a late 17-3 deficit for a home win over South Carolina weeks earlier. Now the Irish were a six-point favorite over Clemson. The game was being broadcast on closed-circuit TV at Littlejohn Coliseum, with tickets going for $9 apiece.

Clemson was terrible in the first half and considered itself lucky to be down just 10-0 at halftime. Notre Dame had 295 yards of offense in the first half, more than the Tigers' dominant defense had allowed in a game all season. The deficit would've been larger had a number of breaks not gone Clemson's way.

After the Tigers trimmed it to 10-6, Bubba Brown had a pulverizing hit that caused a fumble. Davis recovered at the Irish 40, and Lott ran option right for a 26-yard touchdown in the third quarter that put the Tigers up.

Clemson left South Bend with a 16-10 victory, and Devine was despondent afterward. "This is the most disappointing loss I have ever suffered as a coach. I have never felt lower in my life." In the previous forty seasons, Notre Dame had lost its final home game just twice. A member of the Irish Radio Network told listeners that day that Clemson ran up the middle on Notre Dame more than any team he could remember. The Tigers had the ball for fifty plays in the second half, compared to twenty-four for the Irish. Terry Kinard, a freshman defensive back destined for greatness, had two interceptions on this day—including one at Clemson's 3-yard line.

By the time Clemson's charter touched down at Greenville-Spartanburg Airport, the Tigers had decided to accept a bid to the Peach Bowl. Some players were disappointed that the Gator Bowl, considered a higher-profile destination, wasn't more interested in the Tigers after playing host to them the previous two seasons.

The Tigers had to gather themselves quickly. A trip to Columbia awaited, and some people were saying it was the toughest ticket in the history of the Clemson-South Carolina football rivalry. The number thirteen Tigers were facing the number nineteen Gamecocks, led by powerful running back George Rogers, and the *State* labeled it "the irresistible force (USC) against the immovable object (Clemson)."

Since a 56-20 drubbing at the hands of South Carolina in 1975, Clemson had beaten the Gamecocks by scores of 28-9 in 1976, 31-27 in 1977 and 41-23 in 1978. The Tigers' senior class was hoping to become the first class at Clemson since the Second World War to win four in a row over South Carolina.

The Gamecocks had won seven of ten games, and a week earlier, Wake Forest coach John Mackovic labeled them a "great team" after his Demon Deacons suffered a 35-14 loss. South Carolina's staple on offense was a pitch sweep to Rogers, a play that was producing more than 7 yards an attempt. Rogers ranked second in the NCAA in rushing with 144 yards per game and had surpassed 100 yards in his previous eight games.

Ford hadn't been in the Palmetto State long, but already he had a keen sense of the rivalry's importance. He'd been a part of the annual wars between Alabama and Auburn and knew this feud wasn't far behind.

"Coaching really means less in this game than for any other game of the year," he told reporters. "The players all know what the game means, and getting ready to play is never a problem."

The 56,887 fans present at Williams-Brice Stadium that day—plus the estimated 16,500 people who poured into both schools' respective basketball coliseums to watch the game on closed-circuit television—were treated to a classic. Neither team committed a turnover. South Carolina scored a touchdown with four seconds left in the first half. And when Gamecocks punter Jay Feltz boomed a punt eighty-three yards to pin Clemson deep in its own territory with 2:15 left, it appeared the Tigers were done.

But two years after Steve Fuller engineered a heart-stopping drive that culminated with Jerry Butler's unforgettable touchdown catch in Columbia, the Tigers were on the verge of a similar feat after Lott guided them 88 yards on 11 plays to set up a first-and-goal from the 8.

On fourth down from the 5, a Lott throw for Perry Tuttle in the end zone—the same end zone where Butler plucked Fuller's pass from the sky two years earlier—sailed over Tuttle's head, and the Tigers lost 13-9. Ford walked over to console Tuttle after the play.

Lott told reporters after the game that Tuttle was covered well. "The pass had to be perfect, and it wasn't. I threw it too far."

Ford credited South Carolina's defensive back for knocking Tuttle off his pattern to throw the play off. He said an inability to control both lines of scrimmage cost Clemson the game.

"If I had one thing I could do differently, we would have practiced with crowd noise during the week," he said in his postgame press conference. "The noise bothered us a little. I'm not complaining about it at all. It's just that we should have prepared our kids for it better."

Carlen wasn't fond of Ford's predecessor. After Clemson's wins over the Gamecocks in 1977 and 1978, he denigrated the accomplishment by saying Pell won with Red Parker's players. He had no such disdain for Ford after this game.

"We beat a good team," Carlen said. "I applaud Danny Ford and Clemson…Danny Ford did a great coaching job this season."

That was the consensus of media who did not anticipate eight wins from Ford's first team. Herman Helms, columnist for the *State*, wrote this after the Gamecocks' victory:

"Danny Ford may be second-guessed for some of the plays he called in the final frantic seconds Saturday, but the young fellow is deserving of high marks in his first season as head coach at Clemson."

Ford and his players warily
watch Baylor's mascot during
the 1979 Peach Bowl in Atlanta.
*Courtesy of Clemson University Sports
Information Department.*

Ford's 1979 team suffered a fourth loss in the Peach Bowl against Baylor, falling 24-18. Fulton County Stadium was filled with orange-clad fans who came expecting Clemson to close the season in style, but Baylor blocked two punts to jerk momentum from the Tigers' grasp. When the Bears scored a touchdown late in the first half on a desperation heave to the end zone, the odds seemed stacked against Clemson on this day.

The Tigers trimmed the deficit to six with a late touchdown and then recovered an onside kick to trigger hope of a miracle. But a Lott pass was intercepted to end the season on a sour note.

"Our seniors have done an awful lot for this university and the football program," Ford said after the game. "It hurts to lose two games back to back. But if you can't protect the punter you aren't going to beat a whole lot of people."

Ford was still dissecting the bowl loss in the bowels of Fulton County Stadium, but already he had his mind on recruiting.

"We are just going to have to get out there and get some more good players because we don't have a single junior on our offensive football team. We are going to be in a rebuilding situation next year, and spring will be a good time for us. To have a solid program, you just have to have good recruiting years back to back for quite a while, and we haven't done that yet. But we're working on it."

Chapter 3
1980

The winter and spring of 1980 were eventful for Danny Ford as he tried to sustain the success of the three previous seasons.

Ford lost his offensive coordinator when Jimmye Laycock left to become head coach at William & Mary. Defensive line coach Mike Bugar joined former Tigers coach Charley Pell at Florida. Ford brought in Nelson Stokley from Virginia Tech to run the offense. He replaced Bugar with Frank Orgel, who came from East Carolina.

Ford and his staff spent much of winter and spring practice distracted by the exhilarating but exhausting drama of the Herschel Walker sweepstakes. Walker, an almost otherworldly high-school running back from Wrightsville, Georgia, was regarded as the top recruit in the country. He opted against making his choice on signing day in December, instead delaying his announcement until Easter Sunday.

Georgia and Clemson were regarded as the front-runners. Ford told people it would be difficult to snare Walker from the clutches of his home-state Bulldogs, but he said the Tigers had a chance.

In late March, Walker told the Atlanta *Constitution* he was tired of the bickering between Georgia and Clemson. He was so annoyed that he called coaches from Southern Cal and UCLA to tell them the Trojans and Bruins were back in the picture. Al Adams, who covered Clemson for the *Orange and White*, wrote that Walker "might well wind up on the West Coast."

With Easter Sunday approaching, Clemson, Georgia and Georgia Tech agreed to give Walker a few days of peace as he came to his decision. The truce didn't last long; it was rumored to have been broken when a Clemson businessman from North Augusta drove to Wrightsville to talk with Walker. Some people said Georgia assistant Mike Cavan ruined the agreement by trying to sneak a visit with Walker.

Georgia, which finished 6-5 the year before, desperately needed Walker after losing Peach State backs George Rogers (to South Carolina) and James Brooks (to Auburn) in previous years. Walker signed with the Bulldogs.

"I want to be close to home," he said on Easter Sunday. "And Georgia's criminology department will enable me to become an FBI agent like several of my relatives."

In a 2011 interview with Tigerillustrated.com, Ford said the Tigers' staff probably wasn't wise in devoting so much time to recruiting Walker.

"We weren't going to get him. Georgia wasn't going to let us get him. I remember flying down there, playing basketball with him in the gym during P.E. I remember going in his home. And he probably legitimately considered us. But if you knew then what you know now, to pull a player like that out of Georgia, it's almost impossible. I do think we confused him enough to where it made Georgia nervous. But in the end they knew they were going to get him."

Sophomore Homer Jordan was considered the leader in the quarterback race heading into summer, but Andy Headen and Mike Gasque weren't far behind. At a July media gathering in North Carolina, Ford said he hoped his starting quarterback would be a freshman or sophomore "so we don't have to rebuild every year."

The ACC was full of young coaches. Monte Kiffin was in his first year at N.C. State, as was Bill Curry at Georgia Tech. Red Wilson was in his second year at Duke, as were Dick Crum at North Carolina and John Mackovic at Wake Forest. Maryland, led by ninth-year coach Jerry Claiborne, was picked to win the ACC largely because of its great defense.

The Tigers' offense did not have a senior on its two-deep to start the 1980 season. Ford told reporters over the summer that there wasn't

Ford views practice from near the top of a tower at the practice fields on Clemson's campus. *Courtesy of Clemson University Sports Information Department.*

much depth anywhere on the squad, and he fretted about the youth and experience on the offensive line.

At this time, Clemson's rivals in Columbia were getting most of the in-state publicity. People were saying it was the best Gamecock team ever, and Rogers was considered a Heisman candidate before the season began.

Clemson beat Rice 19-3 in the opener, but it was not pretty. The Tigers fumbled six times and lost four of them. Ford lamented "missed assignments, missed tackles, dropped passes and a whole mess of other stuff," but he was confident that his team would play much better the next week at Georgia.

The Bulldogs were ranked number nine after wins over Tennessee and Texas A&M, and it didn't take Walker long to make a splash. He'd already rushed for five touchdowns and 229 yards, and he supplied some crucial running in the come-from-behind victory over the Volunteers in Knoxville.

Ford viewed this matchup in Athens as a measuring stick for Clemson's program. The headliners who'd led the Tigers to so much success in 1977 and 1978 were long gone, and now a bunch of unproven players were under the microscope.

At halftime, Clemson's players and coaches walked into the Sanford Stadium locker room trying to figure out how they were down 14-10. They had a 16-0 first-down advantage, held the ball for more than twenty-five minutes and limited Georgia to just ten offensive plays.

Scott Woerner saw to it that none of those numbers mattered. Less than two minutes into the game, the Bulldogs' defensive back returned a punt sixty-seven yards for a touchdown. Later in the first quarter, Clemson drove deep into Georgia territory and was threatening to score when Jordan threw for Perry Tuttle in the end zone. Woerner intercepted the pass and took it ninety-eight yards the other way to set up a touchdown that put the Tigers down 14-0.

Clemson missed out on two touchdown opportunities in the final seven minutes of the game. Tuttle dropped a pass in the end zone, leading to a field goal that trimmed the margin to 20-16. With two minutes left, the Tigers' final chance evaporated when Jeff Hipp intercepted a tipped pass by Gasque at Georgia's one-yard line.

Walker had just 12 rushing yards in the first half but finished with 121 on 23 carries. Clemson fans were deflated after watching the Tigers lose a game they had dominated, yet Ford seemed optimistic. The Bulldogs were not viewed as a great team at the time, but they went on to claim the national title.

"We improved 200 percent over last week," Ford said after the game. "I think our guys played their pants off. But we gave them too many big plays. Ten years from now, all people will remember is the score, not the stats."

The Tigers won their next three games but had to sweat out each of them—17-10 over Western Carolina, 13-10 over Virginia Tech and 27-24 at Virginia.

Ford was not happy after the Western Carolina victory. He knew the Tigers would have to play much better against the Hokies and

Cavaliers, and he thought his players hadn't shown the physicality and nastiness he desired.

Ford also didn't like fan support against Western Carolina, criticizing the benign atmosphere that in his mind contributed to the indifferent showing on the field. He urged fans to come to the Virginia Tech game wearing "orange outfits" and showing a "positive attitude."

"This team needs fan support. We've got a bunch of seventeen- and eighteen-year-olds, and I really don't know of but one sure thing that motivates them, and that's the recognition of those people in the stands. Our players need our fans to make Clemson a tough place to play, and right now Clemson isn't a very tough place to play."

An estimated crowd of sixty-two thousand fans heeded Ford's calls and created a raucous environment for Virginia Tech. The game was interrupted fourteen times because of the crowd noise at Death Valley. The noise cost Clemson a timeout at one point, and Hokies coach Bill Dooley spent part of his postgame press conference railing on the volume created by Tiger faithful.

The noise cost Dooley's team five yards on a procedure penalty late in the game with the Hokies inside Clemson's ten-yard line, right below the Tigers' student section on the east end of the stadium. Clemson's defense made two big stops in the fourth quarter with Virginia Tech threatening to score the go-ahead touchdown.

Ford was diplomatic about the noise issue, saying each team should be able to hear the signals from its quarterback. But he was pleased that Clemson fans created the imposing environment he requested.

"I'd like to build another side of that stadium over there so we could have some more," he told reporters after the game. "This is the first week they've been excited. Ask anybody who's been around here. It's been a ghost walk the last two weeks."

With three quarters gone at Virginia and the Tigers facing a fourteen-point deficit, Ford was already thinking about what he'd say to the press after becoming the first Clemson coach to lose to the Cavaliers. The Tigers scored a touchdown on the first play of the quarter, blocked a punt for another touchdown and Obed Ariri grooved a fifty-two-yard field goal with eleven seconds left to seal a nerve-jangling 27-24 victory.

After somehow extending Clemson's winning streak over Virginia to twenty games, Ford wasn't quite sure what to say. "I guess they're just going to be the kind of people who make mistakes and then when they have to do it, they do it," he told the press.

At this point in the season, Ford's team was dealing with an assortment of injuries. Fullback Jeff McCall missed several games with a shoulder injury. Four players didn't make the Virginia trip: tight end Bubba Diggs (elbow), receiver Frank Magwood (ankle), defensive back Anthony Rose (knee) and punter David Sims (knee).

Ford also had headaches and frustrations that extended far beyond the injury list. The coach was angry when the *Orange and White*—an independent Clemson newsletter not affiliated with the athletics department—published a lengthy article reporting that at least ten players had left the team.

Ford also wasn't happy with Georgia radio play-by-play man Larry Munson. At a Greenville Touchdown Club function, Munson told the crowd he wanted to thank South Carolina for turning Clemson in to the NCAA for the Tigers' illegal recruiting "of that back from south Georgia," presumably Herschel Walker.

"Georgia also wants to thank North Carolina and North Carolina State for already turning Clemson in to the NCAA," Munson said.

Munson later said his comments "were only in jest." South Carolina coach Jim Carlen blasted Munson and denied that the Gamecocks had turned Clemson in. Carlen said he wanted to call Ford but could not because of the schools' "competitive bitterness."

The Gamecocks had recruited Walker until November 1979, when they pulled out because of their belief that Walker wanted to remain in his home state. Clemson president Bill Atchley said he hoped the allegations were not true because "I don't think we need that kind of" turmoil between the Tigers and Gamecocks.

In December 1979, when the recruitment of Walker was at its most intense, Munson said on an Atlanta TV station that Clemson was being "overly aggressive" in its recruiting of Walker. He also alleged that Clemson and Walker's high school coach were "preparing a package deal" to get Walker to Clemson. The claims were denied by Clemson and Walker's coach.

Munson's latest Clemson-themed allegations were major news the week of the Virginia game, and Ford was still fielding questions about them the next week as he prepared for a visit from Duke. He said he knew of no investigation of Clemson or complaints filed against it. Bulldogs coach Vince Dooley told reporters that Munson was an independent newsman "who is in no way connected to the university." He said he would "sit down with" Munson to resolve the issue.

Ford was angry that he had to spend time answering questions from recruits and their families about this claim instead of devoting his focus to preparing his team. This is what he said on a segment he taped for his pregame radio show that ran before the Duke game:

> *I think anytime when a guy can go out and make a statement and act like he knows what he's talking about, and he's not even involved in football, then he ought to be banned from doing whatever he's doing. I think we're the only team that's giving some team problems recruiting, and I think we're the only one that's giving them problems playing football and they look at it like, "Well, now we've got to do something to stop it."*

A Clemson fan in Georgia wrote to Clemson athletics director Bill McLellan expressing concern over Munson's allegations. McLellan wrote back saying that Dooley informed him Munson would be reprimanded. He also told the fan that Munson called Ford and apologized, saying it was all in jest.

"I feel we at Clemson are bigger than these people who cause controversy and by ignoring them we serve our purpose in a more refined way," McLellan wrote to the fan. "There are always some individuals who strive to cause problems and since we have not done these things we are accused of, it is not necessary to give credence to their comments."

The Tigers were 4-1 entering the Duke game, and Ford believed his team might be on the verge of putting everything together. Instead, sixty thousand stunned fans at Death Valley witnessed an unraveling that completely changed the tenor of the season and left people wondering why Clemson promoted a young offensive line coach to run the program.

Clemson squandered a 17-13 halftime lead and lost 34-17 as a Blue Devils offense coordinated by Steve Spurrier and quarterbacked by Ben Bennett sliced through Clemson's defense. Duke's defense intercepted four passes. Defensive back Dennis Tabron had three of them, including an eighty-seven-yard return for a touchdown. Clemson had ten penalties for eighty-six yards and was docked for six personal fouls. Duke went on to finish 2-9.

"The best team won the game," Ford said afterward. "We've been living on borrowed time for a while now—and it ran out today."

Fans filled the exits with about ten minutes left in the game, provoking this passage from Cobb Oxford in the *Tiger*, Clemson's student newspaper: "If the Tigers are getting pounded, the fans will get up and head for the exits early. Tiger fans always like to pin this trait on South Carolina fans, but the Clemson faithful are just as guilty. They can find the exit just as fast as anybody else if Clemson is losing."

Two days after the Duke debacle, Ford spoke at the Greenville Touchdown Club and told fans not to jump ship just yet and that "we may surprise you."

A day later, at his weekly media luncheon, Ford said that the Tigers' coaching staff had become too soft on players over the course of the season. He said the team "goofed around" but played well enough to win during the 4-1 start, but he vowed to take a more hard-line approach the rest of the year. He also committed to simplifying the offense.

"From now on, we're going to line up and say 'This is it, we're coming at you.' Last year (fans) said that kind of offense was boring, but we're fixing to go back to it. The percentages say it works. You try to do what your people let you do. But you can't let people dictate doing what you don't believe in."

A shortage of offensive line recruits several years earlier was catching up to the Tigers in 1980, and the lack of seniors didn't help either. The starting twenty-two featured just four of them.

Letters from angry fans began to hit McLellan's desk. Hugh Edmonds of Greenville wrote to McLellan on October 19, a day after the Duke loss: "I am afraid that all we have gained over several years is in danger of being lost. There seems to be something very wrong with our football program. It appears that the team has gotten worse instead of better as the season progresses. What it took four or five years to build can be lost in only one."

Charles O'Cain of Inman wrote this letter to the editor of the *Orange and White*:

> *Clemson fans, we're all down, believe you me. But the players aren't the ones to be faulted. The coaching staff has been simply sickening... Coach Ford is still considered a rookie coach and many have written off his mistakes as inexperience. But week after week, he continues to point out his glaring mistakes saying that things will get better next week. Next week, next year seems to remind me of those folks from Columbia. Next week is now and if Danny Ford and his coaching staff don't wake up soon, fans and players alike will soon lose all respect for the 1980 Clemson football team.*

Jimmy Owens, Clemson class of 1966, wrote McLellan and warned that the Tigers were tumbling back to obscurity after winning twenty-seven games in 1977, 1978 and 1979.

> *Please get us a coaching staff for our football players before we waste the last three years of progress. Errors and mistakes have cost our team several games, but yet each week we see the same players in the same positions. This shows a lack of coaching...The offensive portion of his staff is terrible and totally lacking in imagination and guidance. Even I can predict what plays we will run nine out of ten times...All the problems I can see are strictly related to coaching or the lack of it. I believe that it will be hard to get 60,000 people to pay to watch future editions of the Tigers if these problems are not corrected.*

The next week, Clemson went to N.C. State and lost 24-20 after fumbling five times (losing three) and throwing two interceptions. The Tigers out-rushed the Wolfpack 180-147, ran eighty-five plays to State's fifty and had a 19-8 advantage in first downs.

One embarrassing sequence in Raleigh summed up the Tigers' struggles: Clemson recovered a fumble on its own five-yard-line, but two plays later, the Tigers fumbled it right back and the Wolfpack capitalized with a touchdown.

Oxford of the *Tiger* called a blocked punt and a dropped punt snap against the Wolfpack "the most inept plays made by a Clemson team since the 1975 squad came through with a 'sparkling' 2-9 slate."

The next week, interest in the Tigers' next game at Wake Forest was overshadowed by a mammoth showdown in Athens between Georgia and South Carolina, featuring Heisman contenders Herschel Walker and George Rogers. The Bulldogs were putting together a dream season after their narrow victory over Clemson in the second game, and the Gamecocks had the look of an emerging power.

Fuller Howle of Hartsville wrote to McLellan:

> *Bill, how in the hell can we think positively when we are having so many negative coaching decisions. The complaint heard most is Danny's penchant for going for field goals. The State game is a perfect case in point. We take the opening kickoff and drive eighty hard down the field and then kick a field goal on fourth and less than one on the two yard line.*

In Winston-Salem, Clemson managed to squander almost all of a 35-7 lead in the final thirteen minutes after Ford sent in the third string. After reeling off 26 straight points, the Deacons recovered their second onside kick in less than a minute and had a chance to send Clemson to one of the worst defeats in its history. An interception by Terry Kinard preserved a 35-33 victory.

After the game, Ford barred *Orange and White* reporters from conducting interviews of his players, saying some of the recent stories were too negative for a publication that he believed should've been more supportive. He relented a week later after meeting with the reporters, allowing them back inside the Tigers' locker room.

Ford took the blame for inserting the reserves too early against Wake Forest. That didn't stop the letters to McLellan.

From Jones Bolt, Class of 1942:

> *I am not prone to write letters of criticism but this time I just can not hold back. How in the world Danny Ford could have been so dumb to*

blow a 35-7 lead in the fourth quarter against Wake Forest is incredible. And it was Ford and no one else for not pulling the young and relatively inexperienced players as soon as Wake Forest got 14 points…To leave them in there as long as he did was the most flagrant ineptness of a football coach I have seen in along (sic) time.

From Manuel Fernandez of Elberton, Georgia:

I still feel that we do not have enough know how or experience on our staff and that eventually in order to have any kind of strong program, drastic changes must come. We are back to those times when anyone that lines up in front of us can take advantage of us. It doesn't look to me that our youth is hurting us. In my opinion it is a lack of leadership and poor coaching.

North Carolina visited Death Valley a week later and went up big before Clemson trimmed an eighteen-point deficit to five. The Tigers had a first-and-goal from the Tar Heels' one-yard line with less than a minute left, but on third down Lawrence Taylor came from the right side and threw Homer Jordan for a nine-yard loss.

Jordan was pressured on fourth down and threw incomplete, ending the Tigers' hopes of pulling off an upset. The Tar Heels went on to finish 11-1. Ford said after the game that he was "very, very proud" of his team, which dropped to 5-4 with games remaining against Maryland and South Carolina.

Jordan was blossoming as a sophomore, and Ford said fans and media had been too hard on his quarterback. The Tigers' problems with injuries continued: Kinard suffered a broken arm against North Carolina and was out for the year; Tuttle suffered bruised ribs and a bruised shoulder; and defensive back Eddie Geathers suffered a sprained knee.

A week later at Maryland, a Peach Bowl representative was present and ready to offer a bid to Clemson if the Tigers won. But then the game started and Clemson suffered a 34-7 lashing, leaving the Tigers needing to beat South Carolina in their regular-season finale to avoid their first losing season since 1976.

The rumors about Ford's job security intensified as Ford and his staff prepared for a game almost everyone thought they'd lose. The

Gamecocks rolled into Death Valley as an eight-point favorite, and some of Clemson's assistants believed they'd be fired if the Tigers lost.

The night before the game, Ford blasted the rumors about his resignation when a reporter from the *Greenville News* called. Some fans speculated that he was going to bolt to Florida and join Charley Pell, the man who abruptly left Clemson in December 1978 a day after saying he wasn't going anywhere. Fans were still scarred by Pell's abandonment, and not even the craziest rumor seemed implausible less than two years after that traumatic episode.

"It's the most ridiculous thing I've ever heard in my life," Ford told the *News*. "I would never leave Clemson on my own. I'm surprised that our people would believe something like that that other people started."

At the team hotel in Anderson on Saturday morning, Ford interrupted the team breakfast by standing up and telling his players that he had something to say. Some players thought he was about to break the news that he was leaving Clemson. Ford pulled out a pair of orange pants and said that's what they'd wear against the Gamecocks. The room erupted.

The plan, concocted weeks earlier by equipment manager Len Gough, ended up working when Clemson pulled off a 27-6 upset of the number fourteen Gamecocks by pulling away in the second half.

In 2011, Ford told Tigerillustrated.com that his team "needed something extra for motivation."

"That year, they were better than we were...Everybody has tried different things. We just didn't have much to hang our hat on because we were 5-5. It just sounded like a good idea."

At halftime, with the game still close, McLellan was approached by reporters and pressed about Ford's job security. Ford still had three years left on a four-year contract.

"Danny is the coach and will be the coach. I'm sorry these rumors got started, but it happens sometimes when you aren't 9-2 on the season. We think we've got to have continuity around here to be consistently successful, and you can't have continuity when you change coaches."

McLellan noted that the Tigers went into the South Carolina game without twelve injured players who started earlier in the season. Add to that the overall inexperience of Ford's second team, and McLellan believed the struggles were explainable and forgivable.

After a brief celebration with his players, Ford was incensed as he walked into his postgame press conference under the west end zone stands. He opened by saying he was going to hold a press conference at 4:30 to announce his resignation.

And then, after a few seconds of suspenseful silence: "If any of you believe that, you can stick it."

Sunday morning, the Anderson *Independent-Mail* ran a column from sports editor Gerald Garrett with a headline: "And Now (Maybe) The Rumors Will Be Ended."

Wrote Garrett:

> *It comes as no surprise that Ford was upset about the continued operation of the Clemson rumor mill, which already this season has churned out stories about reported NCAA investigations of the Tiger football program (thank Georgia play-by-play announcer Larry Munson for that one), player dissatisfaction and open rebellion against the tactics Ford reportedly used in practice, and now, the resignation stories.*

On his Sunday coach's show with Jim Phillips, Ford was still seething when the tapes began rolling.

"I don't think we made an excuse the whole year, because we don't really believe in excuses. And we've got a bunch of them if we need them…But we don't need excuses, and we've got a lot of things going on good at Clemson. First of all, one of our coaches left last night to go recruiting. And there ain't nobody else in the country that left on a Saturday night to go recruiting, but he's out recruiting."

Ford's last words on the show: "I'll be here next year, Jim. You can bet on that."

Chapter 4
1981

O n March 31, 1981, the *Greenville News* ran a small item on the front of its sports page reporting that two representatives from the NCAA had visited Clemson's campus the previous weekend.

The report followed several weeks of rumors about an NCAA investigation, and university president Bill Atchley responded to the news with a statement acknowledging that the NCAA's visit centered on the signing of two football prospects from Knoxville, Tennessee.

Atchley did not identify the two prospects, but it didn't take long for them to be revealed as quarterback Terry Minor and linebacker James Cofer, both of Rule High School in Knoxville. They had signed letters of intent with Clemson in December but were now asking to be released so that they could sign with other schools. There were reports that Tennessee turned in Clemson to the NCAA, presumably angry about losing two hometown players who'd initially expressed interest in playing for the Volunteers.

Minor and Cofer had signed ACC letters of intent with Clemson but refused to sign national letters of intent. At the time, the conference letter of intent was considered a binding agreement by the ACC and SEC.

Amid the growing volume of headlines and chatter about the NCAA's inquiry, Danny Ford tried to focus on football as his team went through spring practice. A jolting upset of South Carolina in the 1980 regular-season finale had calmed down fans who'd blasted Ford during the second half of a 6-5 campaign, and now Ford looked to his third full season with realistic hopes of ushering the Tigers back to the prominence they enjoyed in 1977, 1978 and 1979.

In February, Ford lost his secondary coach when Mickey Andrews left to join Charley Pell at Florida. Andrews, who came to Clemson after the 1976 season, was the fourth Tigers assistant to join Pell after Pell's abrupt departure from Clemson to Gainesville in December 1978. Ford also lost defensive line coach Frank Orgel, who left to become Auburn's defensive coordinator. Ford brought in Tom Harper from Virginia Tech and made him assistant head coach. Les Herrin, a thirty-two-year-old assistant at Appalachian State, joined the Tigers' staff as linebackers coach.

Players noticed a more consistent leadership style from Ford, who turned thirty-three in April. Star receiver Perry Tuttle, preparing for his senior year, told the *Orange and White* during February's winter conditioning workouts that Ford "is maturing as a head coach and growing with his players."

"Our goals are well established this year," Tuttle said. "We know what to expect."

In the 1983 book *The Clemson Tigers: From 1896 to Glory*, Ford reflected on his growth between the 1980 and 1981 seasons:

> *I can look back and see I made some kind of mistake just about every day. Not big things necessarily, but things like not stressing a point or not talking enough to a particular player. There were times during the 1980 season when I overreacted. I would worry about every rumor that I heard. I probably worried more about those rumors than I did coaching. The toughest thing to say is, "I failed," and we failed five times in 1980. When you lose, you doubt yourself, your plans, whether the players are playing as best they can. Losing creates doubts like winning creates momentum and confidence.*

Athletics director Bill McLellan was encountering some resistance in his push to add a second upper deck to Memorial Stadium, this one on the north side. The *Tiger*, Clemson's student newspaper, objected to student funds being used to add nineteen thousand more seats to Death Valley.

"Students simply cannot afford another upper deck," read an editorial from April 9, 1981. "And if private businesses and individuals are approached for money, it will interfere with any appeal for contributions for a performing arts center, updated and efficient lab equipment and other areas of academic need."

In late June, when Ford and most of the football staff were on vacation, more NCAA news broke. Cofer was interviewed by the *News-Sentinel* of Knoxville and provided the newspaper with a letter that he sent to ACC commissioner Bob James two months earlier. Cofer alleged violations including contacts from Clemson coaches that vastly exceeded the three-visit limit, as well as "transportation and lodging and promises of material gain."

"I was offered both money and merchandise, including a blanket, shirt, pants, coat, jersey, shoes and a color TV," Cofer was quoted as saying.

The *News-Sentinel* reported that Minor wrote a similar letter to the ACC and that the NCAA "received the same information, probably more." Cofer and Minor alleged that a Clemson alumnus in Knoxville, T.C. "Buck" Breazeale, provided illegal inducements. Cofer told James he was promised a summer job at a construction company in Loudon, Tennessee.

Atchley responded with a statement that said Clemson was aware of the article, but he declined further comment given that the investigation was in progress. He did note that neither Cofer nor Minor qualified for admission to Clemson and had been released from their letters of intent.

Dan Foster, columnist for the *Greenville News*, wrote this about the revelations: "These charges attributed to Cofer, if substantiated, could be devastating." Cindy Powell of the *Tiger* wrote that Clemson's biggest game of the upcoming season was "the football program versus the NCAA."

In August, McLellan sent a letter to IPTAY members urging them to refrain from helping in the recruiting process. "While the intentions of each IPTAY member may be the best in the world, the results can be very detrimental to the athletic program," he wrote.

North Carolina was the preseason favorite in the ACC, but Clemson was considered a threat. The Tigers had ten starters returning from an offense that in 1980 finished third in the ACC in rushing, passing and total offense. Included was quarterback Homer Jordan, who'd broken Steve Fuller's record for total offense in a season as a sophomore in 1980.

The defense, which took a massive dip from the elite status of 1979, was supposed to be much better.

Game Plan magazine ranked Clemson nineteenth nationally and second in the ACC. The magazine's editors wrote:

> *The Tigers are hiding in the weeds ready to pounce on one and all who foolishly get too close. Jordan and Co. should roll for averages of 400 yards and four TDs per game, as Clemson's well-balanced attack will give enemy coaches numerous headaches and upset stomachs. Defensively, the Tigers will be absolutely vicious to opposing ball carriers, and enemy passers won't like what happens to them, either. Put it all together and you'll obviously conclude that Clemson's gonna put it to a helluva lot of people before this season is history.*

When a group of ACC sportswriters stopped in Clemson to get a read on the Tigers a few weeks before the start of the season, Ford couldn't hide his optimism. "We've got good people," he said. "I can't deny that."

In a 2011 interview with Tigerillustrated.com, Ford said he knew his team would be better in 1981 because so many players had "grown up" in 1980.

> *The reason we had some experience now is because those kids had the mess beat out of them the year before…You just grow up and you get tired of losing. Once you get a program where you need to have it through recruiting and you keep your numbers straight, and you don't miss on many in recruiting, then you should always have a pretty good program at Clemson. Because they've got everything else. Then again, though, we got caught in that year [1980]. Now they're older, more experienced.*

When the players showed up at Death Valley for fan appreciation day in August, they were wearing all-orange uniforms. Sports information director Bob Bradley told reporters it was the largest turnout ever for the event.

Ford visited the Anderson Area Chamber of Commerce as the season approached and expressed optimism about the present and future. "Mr. McLellan does a good job and lets the people have the best they can have.

And we're fortunate to have a president, Dr. Bill Atchley, who is very interested in athletics. This is by far the most exciting school I've been with. I just hope I do what I need to do to stay here—win football games."

Seven minutes into the opener against Wofford, Clemson hadn't touched the ball and was down 3-0. The Tigers turned things around and won 45-10.

The next game was at Tulane, and eight thousand Clemson fans made the trip to the Big Easy to watch the Tigers win 13-5. Clemson was up 7-5 at the half and used two Bob Paulling field goals in the fourth quarter to create the final margin. Tulane committed seven turnovers and stayed close, yet afterward, Green Wave coach Vince Gibson said his team was "physically whipped" by the Tigers, who started 2-0 for the first time since 1970.

Two lost fumbles and an assortment of mental mistakes bothered Ford, but he was happy to leave the Superdome with a victory. "Anytime you win and make as many errors as we did, you have to feel thankful to get out alive," he told reporters afterward. "But they were little 'ole bitty things we can correct."

Clemson had no problems shifting its focus to Georgia, which entered Death Valley still high from its 1980 national championship. The Tigers were still steamed about a four-point loss in Athens in the second game of 1980, a game Clemson dominated statistically.

"Clemson totally outplayed us last year, but we got more points," Georgia coach Vince Dooley told reporters at his Tuesday press conference. "They feel like Georgia is responsible for what they feel was a bad season. Clemson has been waiting 365 days for this game."

At his own press conference, Ford talked about the budding Clemson-Georgia rivalry. The Bulldogs owned a 33-13-3 advantage in the series, but the Tigers had knocked them off in 1974, 1977 and 1979.

The number four Bulldogs brought in a fifteen-game winning streak that the Tigers gleefully shattered in a 13-3 victory. Georgia committed nine turnovers, including five interceptions by Buck Belue, and star tailback Herschel Walker fumbled three times and lost two—including one at Clemson's thirteen-yard line on Georgia's second possession.

Walker, who came close to signing with Clemson in April 1980, told reporters that the noise at Death Valley affected his concentration. Defensive end Jeff Bryant said he saw Walker nervously glancing at

Clemson defenders instead of focusing on the ball before he lost a fumble on an exchange with Belue.

Clemson's players puffed victory cigars in the locker room afterward. The Tigers won in the same orange pants that Ford unveiled to motivate his team before the 1980 upset of South Carolina. Ford initially intended for the pants to be worn only against the Gamecocks, but the seniors convinced him to wear them in this game.

In an interview with the *Orange and White*, offensive line coach Larry Van Der Heyden said Jordan was capable of making precision throws when defenses ganged up to stop the Tigers' running game. "We went into the game with four or five basic plays. They stopped our running game and took away what we thought would be our best play. They forced us to throw, and we took advantage of the passing game. Last year we were in trouble when people took things away from us. But when they shut down the run, they had to contend with Homer on the corner."

The defense's plan was to make Walker run laterally and swarm to him whenever he had the ball. Walker told reporters that the Bulldogs "didn't play like champions" and were rattled by the deafening crowd. "There's always a lot of noise at Clemson, and our coaches told us we couldn't let it distract us. But I'm afraid it did."

Two days after the Tigers' first win over a Top Ten team since 1967, the NCAA investigators were back in town as the team moved into an open week. Atchley told the *Orange and White* that the NCAA wanted to speak with "certain coaches and players."

"If they are to come on campus, this is the time we prefer them to," Atchley said. "It is less disruptive. It gives everyone time to get his mind off this and back on the game."

Atchley maintained that this was still merely a preliminary investigation. "We are not guilty of anything. You are not guilty until a charge comes down." Atchley did say the school would "take our lumps with the rest of them" if violations were discovered. He predicted it would take three or four months for the NCAA to return findings. Ford declined to comment on the investigation, referring all questions to the president's office.

In the next game at Kentucky, Clemson responded after a sluggish first half and won 21-3. The Tigers had just sixty-five yards of offense at halftime.

Wildcats coach Fran Curci said Clemson's defensive line, nasty and powerful thanks in part to massive freshman William Perry, "is the best I've seen." Billy Reed, columnist for the *Courier-Journal* of Louisville, was impressed by the enthusiasm of three thousand Clemson fans who made the trip to Kentucky.

"The Clemson fans yesterday gave the UK fans a more significant lesson than the Clemson players gave the UK players. They not only wore their orange, they yelled and rooted and had a fine old time. Mostly, they cared. They really cared, and they transmitted that to their players…It's tough to win when you're playing in Commonwealth Stadium, and yet the home-field advantage belongs to Clemson."

Through the 4-0 start, Clemson was ranked number one nationally in scoring defense after having allowed a total of twenty-one points. The Tigers amassed twenty-three takeaways (ten fumbles and thirteen interceptions) against just seven turnovers by the offense.

Clemson needed a monster fourth-quarter comeback to beat Virginia in 1980 but had no such trouble this time in Death Valley, moving to 21-0 all-time over the Cavaliers with a 27-0 win. Chuck McSwain and Cliff Austin helped the Tigers total 265 rushing yards.

Virginia coach Dick Bestwick said after the game that Clemson boasted more than just a great defense. The presence of productive running backs, a physical offensive line and Jordan and an elite receiver in Tuttle made the Tigers' offense formidable.

"People criticize their offense, but I don't understand why," Bestwick said. "They don't make any mistakes or turnovers, and they score what it takes to win."

Bestwick also marveled at the Clemson football phenomenon as a whole.

"This is what football should be all about, the way they have it at Clemson. Out at the motel, you don't see a bunch of drunks. You see families there. They have children coming to the football game with their parents, and they have parties like you are supposed to have. This Clemson operation—I can't say anything negative about it. I'd be proud if every school in the country operates like Clemson does."

The Tigers moved into the Top Ten the next week, carrying a number six ranking to Duke. They were 5-0 for the first time since 1948, and fans were starting to think big.

Clemson had no trouble in Durham, taking out some frustration for its embarrassing blowout loss to the Blue Devils a year earlier. The Tigers won 38-10 while piling up 563 yards of total offense.

Clemson rose to number four, the highest ranking in its history, and some people wondered if the Tigers would have trouble focusing on their next two games against N.C. State and Wake Forest with a monstrous showdown at North Carolina looming on November 7.

The Wolfpack stunned the home crowd by going up 7-0 in the first quarter after an Austin fumble on Clemson's third offensive play gave possession to the visitors. The Tigers rebounded and won 17-7, beating N.C. State for just the third time in the previous thirteen meetings. Clemson's defense allowed its first rushing touchdown of the season but held the Wolfpack without a first down from the third play of the second quarter until 7:50 remained in the game.

"We weren't clicking on all twelve volts," Ford said after the game. "But not many teams in the nation are 7-0."

On this day, South Carolina went to number three North Carolina as a two-touchdown underdog and left with a 31-13 victory.

A few days later, former Georgia defensive coordinator Erk Russell angered Clemson fans when he told the newspaper in Athens, Georgia, that the Tigers' win over Georgia was "a fluke." He said if the two teams faced each other twenty times, the Bulldogs would win nineteen times. Russell was in his first year as head coach of Georgia Southern.

Clemson destroyed Wake Forest 82-24, totaling 756 total yards and scoring the first seven times it touched the ball. The Tigers drew some criticism for running up the score, but Deacons coach Al Groh didn't air any grievances. He said he knew before the game it would be a mismatch and told one of his coaches that he wondered if the Deacons would ever be able to stop the Tigers' offense.

"It was our job to stop them, not their job to stop themselves," he said in the postgame press conference. "I thought they were more than gracious... It was a case of putting young little boys out there against big, strong men. We watched five films on Clemson, and we knew they had big, strong aggressive linemen. That's where you build a good football team."

Later in the day, number one Penn State lost to Miami and number two Pitt struggled to beat a mediocre Boston College team. Clemson moved up to number two the next week, and Pitt rose to the top spot. Penn State was the fifth number one team to lose by this point in the 1981 season. The Hurricanes had recently been put on probation and were considered out of contention for the Orange Bowl.

As the Tigers were preparing for the first Top Ten matchup in ACC history, the *Washington Post* dispatched a young reporter named John Feinstein to Clemson to write an investigative story on the Tigers' dream season and the specter of the NCAA investigation.

Two days before Clemson's showdown at North Carolina, the story ran.

"On this idyllic campus where the trees are just now beginning to turn color, there is a darkening cloud on the horizon, one that threatens to engulf Clemson at the very moment when it should be celebrating its greatest athletic achievements."

Feinstein wrote that six coaches and twenty-eight players were questioned on the NCAA's second visit to the campus less than two months earlier, just days after the groundbreaking 13-3 victory over Georgia at Death Valley.

"According to sources at the school, the NCAA is considering as many as 100 charges against Clemson, some of which date back to the previous coaching regime headed by Charley Pell, now at Florida," said the article, which ran November 5.

Feinstein observed in the article that Ford was a "friendly man" who "turns cold at the mention of the NCAA."

"I don't see any cloud hanging over this program, 'cause we haven't done anything wrong," Ford told Feinstein.

McLellan to Feinstein: "I would never say flatly that we're lily white, because I can't keep track of every move made in this department. I don't think anyone on our level can. But our coaches are men of integrity. I don't believe they would ever blatantly break the rules."

One unidentified staff member told Feinstein that the NCAA investigation was "all the kids were talking about" at the start of practice in August. "We had to face it," the staffer said. The players were told to go through the season as if nothing at all was going on between the NCAA and Clemson, the article said.

Feinstein asked Ford about the magical season that was unfolding. Just three years earlier, Pell left Clemson for Florida because he believed he could win a national title with the Gators.

"Sometimes, I catch myself thinking, 'Can it really happen at Clemson?'" Ford told Feinstein. "And the answer is, of course it can. Then I smile for a second and go back to work."

Feinstein asked Ford what came to his mind when he thought of the NCAA investigation. His reply: "I think, there's nothing wrong with our football program for a second, and then I go back to work."

President Atchley declared Thursday "Danny Ford Day" at the university. Ford was honored during a pep rally at the university amphitheater the night before the football team departed for Chapel Hill. An estimated two thousand fans showed, as did an entourage from Ford's hometown of Gadsden, Alabama.

North Carolina rebounded from the blistering loss to South Carolina with a 17-10 win at Maryland the week earlier to vault back into the Top Ten, but the 7-1 Tar Heels limped in with injuries to quarterback Rod Elkins and tailback Kelvin Bryant. A record 130 writers and broadcasters requested credentials to cover a game that ABC was beaming to 60 percent of the country.

Clemson earned an emotional 10-8 win in Chapel Hill by stifling the Tar Heels' prolific offense. North Carolina entered the game averaging 430 yards a game and finished with just 263. The Tigers were unsuccessful running the option outside but countered with a pounding running game between the tackles. The offensive line opened holes for Jeff McCall and Kevin Mack, who combined for 123 yards on twenty-five carries.

Defensive tackle Jeff Bryant fell on a pass-turned-lateral at the North Carolina twenty-five with fifty-seven seconds left, and the number two Tigers moved ever closer to an Orange Bowl bid while improving to 9-0.

Ford didn't show much exuberance after the game. Outside, in the Kenan Stadium stands, thousands of Clemson fans continued to celebrate well after the game's conclusion.

"We don't deserve number one, because we didn't play well today," Ford told reporters. "And we had way too many turnovers. We are not ready for number one. We still have two more ball games to play and we have to get ready."

The next week, news broke that ABC's Jim Lampley had interviewed Cofer and Minor two days before the North Carolina game. ABC had planned to air the interview during the game broadcast, but it opted against it after Clemson's administration refused to provide a response to the allegations. Ford was quoted by the *Washington Post* saying the Tigers wouldn't have taken the field in Chapel Hill had ABC aired the interview before the game.

Associate athletics director Bobby Robinson told the *Greenville News* that ABC contacted Clemson on Friday when the Tigers were going through their walk-through at Kenan Stadium.

"We told them we would not respond to the interviews. My point was that we had not been charged with anything, that there was no reason for them to put it on the air, that they had never interviewed any athlete like that and put it on the air. They said the decision came from New York, and I said, 'Well, tell me who to call in New York.'"

The Tigers returned home for a matchup with Maryland that made Ford understandably nervous. The Terps had defeated Clemson eight times in the previous nine seasons, including a 34-7 debacle the previous year. The Tigers dusted off the lucky orange pants for a 21-7 win that clinched the ACC title and kept alive hopes of much more. Jordan carved up the Terps' secondary for thirty completions and 270 passing yards.

Visions of playing for the national title were dancing in the heads of everyone at Clemson, but one obstacle remained: a trip to Columbia to face the hated Gamecocks.

In the joyful locker room after the win over Maryland, linebackers coach George Cain said to the *Orange and White*, "Now if they just keep fighting for the next goal, we can get to the Orange Bowl and maybe the national championship. Our next goal is to beat the (expletive) out of South Carolina down there in Columbia."

The Gamecocks had suffered an ugly loss to Pacific earlier in the season and had to beat Clemson to be considered for a bowl game.

During the week, Clemson fans were wrapped up in Orange Bowl mania. The bowl was already sold out by this point, excepting the allotments that would be distributed to the participating schools. There were no available flights out of Miami until January 4.

The Gamecocks were a mess on offense, averaging just 266 yards a game. It seemed like a mismatch against a Clemson defense giving up a mere 7.7 points per contest. Yet Ford was worried that the Gamecocks would spring the same sort of surprise Clemson pulled off the year before in Death Valley. In that game, South Carolina came in highly regarded and most people expected the Gamecocks to roll over the demoralized Tigers. Clemson won 27-6, and the upset was viewed as a springboard for all the great things being accomplished in 1981. Clemson had lost on its last visit to Williams-Brice Stadium, a 13-9 defeat in 1979.

"There are just too many similarities to last year," Ford told reporters at his Tuesday luncheon. "I don't like it. This game isn't always for the one who's supposed to win...I just hope we look at this game as we should. I don't know how many players have a chance to play for an undefeated team or how many coaches have the chance to coach an undefeated team."

South Carolina began the game on an emotional high and went up 7-0 early. Clemson held a tenuous 15-13 lead in the third quarter, but the Tigers pushed through and pulled away for a 29-13 victory.

Ford and athletics director Bill McLellan speak with Orange Bowl representatives in Columbia on the day Clemson sealed an undefeated regular season with a victory over rival South Carolina. *Courtesy of Clemson University Sports Information Department.*

After pelting the artificial turf with oranges for much of the game, Clemson fans held up bumper stickers that read: "11-0: A chicken kickin' makes it perfect." A newspaper photographed senior linebacker Jeff Davis holding up one of the decals.

For weeks, Ford hesitated to call his team great. He finally gave in on this day. "You have to," he said. "Hell, they're 11-0."

Clemson was bound for an Orange Bowl showdown with Nebraska, a matchup that Tigers strength coach George Dostal posted on a wall the previous summer in a challenge to the team.

Seven days later, Clemson's campus was virtually empty on Thanksgiving weekend when Todd Blackledge and Penn State erupted for 48 straight points in a 48-14 trouncing of number one Pittsburgh, snapping the Panthers' seventeen-game winning streak and assuring that Clemson would rise to number one. Ford was in Birmingham, Alabama, watching from the Legion Field sidelines as sixty-eight-year-old Bear Bryant secured his 315th victory in an Alabama win over Auburn.

Clemson was the lone unbeaten team remaining in college football after Pitt became the sixth number one team to fall. But the celebration was severely tempered by the fallout from ABC's decision to run a lengthy story on the NCAA's investigation at halftime of the Penn State-Pitt game. The story was splashed across the pages of Upstate newspapers Monday morning, making a virtual sidebar of the Tigers' imminent ascent to the top spot.

Clemson was the overwhelming number one in both the Associated Press and United Press International polls. The ACC's only national title to this point had been earned by Maryland in 1953, the conference's first year of existence.

Clemson supporters were enraged at the treatment and timing of the segment, suggesting ABC sought to downgrade Clemson's Orange Bowl matchup against Nebraska (televised by NBC) and promote its own Sugar Bowl showdown between Pitt and Georgia, a game that was going head-to-head with the Orange.

ABC fanned the flames even more by interviewing former Tigers basketball coach Tates Locke, who was then an assistant at University of Nevada, Las Vegas, under Jerry Tarkanian. In the mid-1970s, Clemson was hammered by the NCAA for an assortment of major recruiting violations that occurred under Locke.

Asked by ABC whether he'd be shocked if there was truth to claims of "front money" given to Clemson recruits, Locke responded: "I happen to know that it is prevalent."

Cofer told Lampley that Knoxville businessman T.C. "Buck" Breazeale, a Clemson alumnus, gave him a "Christmas gift" of $1,000 in cash. Cofer said Ford and former assistant coach Billy Ware knew about the gift. Minor told Lampley that Breazeale gave him $500 for Christmas.

McLellan was notified late on the day before Thanksgiving that the eight-minute segment would air Saturday. He spent Friday trying to prevent the airing, even contacting the NCAA. His efforts were unsuccessful.

In an Associated Press report, McLellan said ABC's story was "an unprecedented thing in college athletics, in our opinion."

"I think they were trying to promote the Sugar Bowl instead of the Orange bowl," he said. University president Bill Atchley said ABC's report, which was prompted by Feinstein's investigative piece in the *Washington Post*, was not fair given that the investigation was still in progress and Clemson had not been found guilty of any wrongdoing.

"It's very pathetic," Atchely told reporters. "I wonder why ABC would go to such an extent with us when they haven't done it (with schools charged by the NCAA). It was not a class thing to do and showed poor taste."

Stan Marks, chairman of the Orange Bowl committee, called the report "a cheap shot." "They were trying to do that to help the Sugar Bowl, and I just can't get over it."

Senator Strom Thurmond, a 1923 Clemson graduate, later wrote a letter to Roone Arledge of ABC News calling the report "highly prejudiced and one-sided."

"Without question, ABC was within its rights to air this report," Thurmond wrote, "but Clemson school officials, students, alumni, and supporters are extremely upset at the timing of this telecast and the unfairness with which it was presented."

On December 18, when the Tigers were en route to Florida to begin bowl preparations, Cofer and Minor filed a $12 million lawsuit against Ford, Breazeale, Ware and ACC Commissioner Bob James. They claimed the illegal inducements prevented them from playing for Tennessee, the school they initially intended to attend.

Ford continued to abide by the university's policy of not commenting on the investigation. The strain and pressure of the situation didn't prevent him from enjoying what he and his team accomplished just a year after fans called for his ouster.

Ford was still bitter about some of the things he heard and read toward the end of the 1980 season when his injured and inexperienced team was stumbling down the stretch.

"You learn about people and situations," he said in the Spartanburg *Herald-Journal*. "You think, when you start out in something like this, that you know people. But you don't. The same folks that were saying you couldn't coach last year are the first ones saying you can this year.

"And it ain't a bit of difference this year than it was at this time last year. We were young last year offensively and they weren't ready to play. We played too many young folks and experience means everything in this game. But there are some things about last year I won't ever forget. I know a little bit more about people now. There are some people, people I call zeroes, that I don't want nothing to do with."

Ford did acknowledge in December 1981 that he "hurt the players more than I helped them" in 1980. He believed that a lack of organization and inconsistent leadership contributed to the team's slide. "We lost our poise as coaches and got away from our plans."

The team convened December 19 in New Smyrna Beach, Florida, a small resort near Daytona Beach. The Tigers spent a week there before moving to their headquarters in Miami a week later.

Clemson's players and coaches believed they were being underestimated despite their 11-0 record and top ranking. Nebraska had suffered two losses but was a four-point favorite, and at some pre-bowl functions attended by both teams the Tigers detected arrogance from the Cornhuskers—an unspoken belief that an obscure upstart from a basketball conference shouldn't be able to stay on the field with an established powerhouse from the Big Eight.

A Clemson loss in the Orange Bowl would have enabled a number of teams to stake a claim to the national title. Georgia was perceived to be in the mix, and sophomore tailback Herschel Walker told the media in New

Orleans that the Bulldogs were better than the Tigers despite the beating his team took in Death Valley.

"If we played Clemson again tomorrow, we'd beat them, and really beat them bad," Walker said. "I'm not putting Clemson down, but any team that gets nine turnovers and only beats you 13-3 when it should have been 40-to-something isn't that strong a team."

The media asked Ford to make a case for Clemson winning the national title even with a loss in the Orange Bowl.

"I'd have a hard time convincing someone of anything after getting our butts whipped," he told reporters in Miami. "Anyway, I haven't done any campaigning all year, and I'm not trying to campaign now. All I know is we've played eleven times, and we've whipped eleven folks. And I'd like to do it one more time."

Georgia ended up losing to Pitt in the Sugar. Another contender fell when Bryant and Ford's alma mater lost to Texas in the Cotton.

Then Clemson went out and left no doubt against Nebraska by taking over in the third quarter. The final score was 22-15, but the victory was

Ford shouts instructions during the Orange Bowl against Nebraska. *Courtesy of Clemson University Sports Information Department.*

more decisive than seven points. Powerful running backs Mike Rozier and Roger Craig were each held under 100 yards rushing. The Cornhuskers mustered just 256 yards of offense and were down 22-7 late in the third.

The headline in the *Miami Herald* the next morning read: "Clemson really is a Tiger." Columnist Edwin Pope said the Tigers "terrorized" the Huskers and proved "they were as underrated by the odds as they were truly rated by the polls."

Pete Axthelm of *Newsweek* wrote that the game was "a fluorescent orange blur."

"On both offense and defense, Clemson always seemed a half-dash count quicker than Nebraska." Axthelm raved about William Perry, the freshman who more than held his own against star center Dave Rimington.

"I don't have to argue with somebody who says we got here by cheating," Perry told Axthelm. "Did we have twelve guys out there tonight? No. Both sides used eleven at a time, and we had the best eleven."

Perry's defensive line coach, Willie Anderson, sneered at the people who thought Clemson couldn't hold up. "The kids were sick and tired of hearing people put us down and I think that's one reason we played so well tonight," he told the *Orange and White*. "I've been hearing about Nebraska all week and I just want to say one thing: Clemson is a national power. Quote, unquote."

Jeff Davis, who had fourteen tackles and a fumble recovery in the final game of a brilliant Clemson career, said the Tigers had plenty of motivational fuel entering the game.

"I could tell they were taking us lightly during the week," Davis told the *Orange and White*. "Just being around them during the week, at the Faces Disco in Coconut Grove and out at the stadium, I could tell. Even the way they came out for the game tonight, the way they trotted past—you could feel it in the atmosphere, like 'We're from the Big Eight and you boys aren't the same caliber.'"

Back in Clemson, a crowd estimated at about three hundred people poured out of the bars and celebrated on College Avenue. Trouble started when police tried to stop revelers from jumping onto moving cars. Beer bottles were hurled at the officers, and ten people were arrested.

After a wild celebration at the team hotel, Ford finally got to bed

Ford on the sidelines of the Orange Bowl with head trainer Fred Hoover. *Courtesy of Clemson University Sports Information Department.*

around 4:30 a.m. Less than seven hours later, he showed up at a day-after press conference with Nebraska coach Tom Osborne wearing a button-down shirt, jeans and boots.

Ford revealed that Clemson's game plan was to stay close for three quarters and then win the fourth quarter because of superior conditioning. Osborne said Clemson "dominated the line of scrimmage."

Ford was already thinking about recruiting. The staff was behind in that area after spending a month focused solely on bringing a national title to Clemson.

"You look at Nebraska and see that after getting there, they've stayed here," Ford said. "We're going to find out a lot about our program over the next couple of years."

In his story for *Newsweek*, Axthelm noted the specter of NCAA scrutiny that threatened to taint the Tigers' moment of glory.

"The players seemed almost resigned to an impending probation that may keep them out of the bowls next year. But they insist the NCAA investigation has not distracted them or stamped an asterisk on their title quest."

Ford posing with the Orange Bowl trophy that Clemson brought home after its 22-15 victory over Nebraska. *Courtesy of Clemson University Sports Information Department.*

Clemson's charter arrived January 3 at Greenville-Spartanburg Airport on a cold, rainy day. Ford descended from the plane carrying his seven-month-old daughter, Elizabeth.

Back at the athletics department, receptionist Martha Garrison spent the week answering the switchboard with the following phrase:

"Jervey Athletic Center. Home of the national champions."

Chapter 5

1982

In February 1982, Danny Ford broke his long silence on the NCAA's year-long investigation of Clemson. Ford, a little more than a month removed from guiding the Tigers to the pinnacle of college football, was part of a nine-man coaching panel that met in Kansas City with a group of reporters.

Ford said the NCAA was investigating a "thick" file of complaints from Clemson's competition. "You don't get investigated until you get turned in by so many people, and you get a file so thick," he told reporters.

> *They've done a thorough job on Clemson. But if they did a thorough job on everybody before they got an accusation, they would prevent a lot...I'm taking up for myself, but the head coach knows least of what's going on of anybody in the whole organization. They're not out there in the field, but they're responsible for everybody in the world...I know I've broken some rules, and any coach who says he hasn't is not being truthful with himself.*

This was a time when some people believed big-time college athletics was beginning to spiral out of control as a result of big money allegedly lavished upon coveted recruits. Notre Dame basketball coach Digger Phelps startled many in the winter of 1982 when he said he knew of a number of basketball coaches who were paying a standard rate of $10,000 a year for decorated recruits.

University of Alabama at Birmingham coach Gene Bartow said money was "flowing like water" to top prospects. Penn State's Dick Harter said Phelps's claims were accurate, "but I have felt the price is even higher than $10,000 a year." The *New York Times* reported that Phelps was later congratulated by other coaches who admired his willingness to expose blatant wrongdoing.

In the mid-1970s, the NCAA slapped Clemson's basketball program with probation for major violations committed under Tates Locke. At the time, athletics director Bill McLellan said Clemson would learn from the mistakes that produced those transgressions.

On March 27, 1982, Ford was inducted into the South Carolina Athletic Hall of Fame with Summerville High School football coach John McKissick. Two days later, hours before Michael Jordan made a late shot to lift North Carolina to an NCAA title triumph over Georgetown in New Orleans, the NCAA notified Clemson of an "official inquiry" into its football program.

Clemson was given between thirty days and four months to make a written reply to the NCAA's Committee on Infractions. University president Bill Atchley told reporters that the school would "look into the problems and try to justify them…And if we are guilty, we could get anything from a slap on the wrist to probation."

Dick Young, a columnist for the *New York Post*, reported that Clemson would receive two years of probation. A day after Clemson received notice from the NCAA, Ford told the *Greenville News* it was "business as usual" inside the football program.

In a 2011 interview with Tigerillustrated.com, Ford said two NCAA investigators interviewed him on his boat while he was fishing on Lake Hartwell.

"They'd ask questions and talk, then write it down. After I finished the interview, they showed it to me on paper and I remember asking them to mark out some of the words I used. I didn't want them sending that report to the committee because it was full of ugly words, because I was mad."

Student reporters at the *Tiger* came down hard on the presence of more NCAA scrutiny of Clemson. "It is hard to respect or trust an athletic department that has had its reputation spotted by such an accusation—

Ford poses with his family in the mid-1980s. Clemson moved forward with plans to build Ford a 4,160-foot home after the national title season of 1981. *Courtesy of Clemson University Sports Information Department.*

twice," an editorial read on April 1, 1982. "Worst of all, Clemson's first-ever national championship is now being attributed to illegal recruiting and cheating."

The editorial said the blame "should go to alumni and supporters who apparently believe that a recruit sees dollar signs instead of footballs when they choose a university."

In April, it was announced that Clemson's 1982 game at Georgia would be played at 9:00 p.m. on Labor Day and be televised by ABC. The game was originally scheduled for September 18 at 1:30 p.m., but the national interest in a clash between the previous two national champions led both schools to agree to make it a showcase.

Ford oversees a drill during practice. Ford was known for his devotion to physical play on the offensive and defensive lines. *Courtesy of Clemson University Sports Information Department.*

Georgia hadn't played host to a night game in thirty years, and there were no lights at Sanford Stadium. ABC was offering to pay for temporary lighting, plus $550,000 to each team. Clemson was considering making lighting a part of its stadium expansion that would have a second upper deck ready by the 1983 season. The Tigers hadn't played a night game in twenty-five years and had never played a regular-season game on national television.

The spring game was televised by ESPN and shown on tape delay five times during the first week of May. About six thousand fans showed for the game, braving heavy rains and a muddy field. Ford was presented with the Associated Press national title trophy at halftime and provided commentary for the ESPN broadcast.

The media picked North Carolina to win the ACC in 1982, largely because the Tar Heels had fifteen starters returning from a 10-2 team in 1981. Clemson, which lost eleven starters and had to rebuild its offensive line, received just twelve first-place votes to North Carolina's sixty-one in the preseason voting by ACC media.

Receivers Perry Tuttle and Jerry Gaillard were gone, but quarterback Homer Jordan was back for his senior year. Running backs Cliff Austin and Chuck McSwain also returned.

The defense's biggest losses were Jeff Davis and Jeff Bryant. The defensive line was still powerful thanks largely to the return of William Perry and William Devane on the interior. The two combined for eighty tackles and thirteen sacks in 1981.

Ford was excited about the addition of freshman running backs Kenny Flowers, Terrence Flagler and Stacey Driver.

The demand for tickets was overwhelming. The second upper deck would be ready in 1983, adding fifteen thousand seats and pushing capacity of Memorial Stadium past eighty thousand. But fans were clamoring to attend the six home games in 1982. Clemson purchased an ad in the papers to send a message to the faithful:

"At the Clemson Athletic Department we sincerely appreciate the outstanding support of you, our fans. We regret that we are unable to meet the tremendous demand for tickets. It is our hope that we will be able to enlarge our stadium prior to next season so that you will have an opportunity to see the Tigers play."

The student newspaper continued to criticize the planned construction of a second upper deck, particularly in the midst of university budget cuts.

"We don't deny there is an increased demand for tickets this year, but we feel there are more pressing needs on campus than the addition of 15,000 seats to Memorial Stadium," read an August 26 editorial in the *Tiger*.

> *A new chemistry building tops the list of academic needs that all to (sic) often get lost in the mania of 'Tiger Fever'…It's true that the Tigers are the defending national football champions, but it is also true that they are currently under NCAA investigation. Probation of one sort or another seems imminent. Will fans still turn out in large numbers to see a team that can't win the national championship no matter how good they are? We don't think so.*

As the showdown with Georgia approached in the summer of 1982, the big story was Herschel Walker possibly missing the game with a fractured thumb that he suffered in an August 21 scrimmage. Bulldogs coach Vince Dooley, whose only regular-season blemish the previous two seasons was a 13-3 loss at Clemson in 1981, said a week before the game that Walker would dress out.

"It all hinges on the doctor," the coach told reporters in Athens. "If he says, 'OK, he can play but here are the risks,' then I have a decision to make."

Clemson fans drove to Athens sporting bumper stickers proclaiming the lights would go out in Georgia. As it turned out, the Tigers' offense suffered the power outage in a 13-7 defeat that wasn't as close as the final score indicated.

Walker wore a protective cast and didn't play in the first half, finishing with twenty yards on eleven carries. Jordan threw four interceptions, and the Tigers were three of seventeen on third down. The rebuilding offensive line couldn't protect Jordan, and the Bulldogs blocked a punt.

Ford seemed far from shattered as he reflected on the defeat, and his optimism surprised some observers. The Tigers' ranking dropped from number eleven to sixteen.

Two days after the loss in Athens, the *Greenville News* reported that the purchase of a 1982 Monte Carlo for Jordan had drawn scrutiny in the NCAA's probe of Clemson. Jordan was the first active player whose name had surfaced since the NCAA's investigation began in early 1981.

Atchley made an appearance on "The Today Show" in early September and defended college athletics as a legitimate amateur enterprise. Questioned by Bryant Gumbel on the NCAA investigation of Clemson, Atchley responded: "If we are guilty of some things, we'll stand up and take our medicine and I'll take some steps to correct those. We're already doing that." Over the summer, Atchley had appointed a five-member committee to conduct an in-house investigation at Clemson as the school prepared its response to the NCAA.

The Tigers had a weekend off to prepare for a visit from Boston College, but Ford was apprehensive about the matchup and said the Eagles would be a more difficult foe than Georgia. His fears were realized when Boston College, led by a jitterbug quarterback named Doug Flutie, battled the Tigers to a 17-17 draw in front of a disappointed home crowd.

A week later, Clemson was up just 10-9 on Western Carolina at halftime before sweating out a 21-10 win. The Tigers were outgained 340-317, and afterward Ford called the win a "farce," "an embarrassment" and "the poorest performance that I've ever been associated with."

The next week, as the unranked Tigers prepared to play host to Kentucky, Atchley announced that Clemson was barring Jordan from playing against the Wildcats because of a possible NCAA violation. Jordan's car had been purchased at an Easley automobile dealership owned by an IPTAY member.

Atchley released a statement saying he requested Jordan not play because Clemson was "looking into the purchasing and the financing of Homer Jordan's car."

Quarterback Mike Eppley, the heir apparent at quarterback after the 1982 season, didn't learn he was starting against Kentucky until two days before the game. The Tigers won 24-6 over the Wildcats, who ended up finishing the season winless.

Jordan was back the next week when Clemson went to Virginia and smashed the Cavaliers 48-0 to improve to 3-1-1, but the next week in practice he suffered a knee injury and was taken to the hospital. On the same day, standout defensive tackle Dan Benish went down with a knee injury.

Nine Tigers missed an easy win over Duke with injuries. Jordan underwent arthroscopic surgery two days after the game and had difficulty with his knee for the rest of the season.

Ford's eighteenth-ranked team went to Raleigh the next week and defeated N.C. State 38-29 for its fifth win in a row, but the game wasn't the story on this day. The postgame handshake became a nasty confrontation when Ford accused Wolfpack coach Monte Kiffin of ratting out Clemson to the NCAA. Investigators had visited Raleigh to question N.C. State players who had also been recruited by the Tigers, and Ford believed Kiffin was the whistleblower.

A Raleigh television station picked up parts of the midfield exchange.

Ford: "My ass you didn't turn us in…They have been up here three times."

Kiffin: "I didn't tell them…I didn't tell them."

Ford: "Who did?"

Kiffin: "I never did. I never turned you in…They came up here. I don't know how they got here."

The next week, *Sports Illustrated* ran an item on the argument:

> *Asked about this exchange with Ford, Kiffin at first denied it had taken place but changed his tune when informed that the tape existed. Ford was a bit slippery, too. After first trying to claim that his confrontation with Kiffin had been "a private conversation,"—a curious objection, considering it had occurred amid a milling crowd—Ford said, "Ain't no telling what I said after the game. But if I said it, I said it."*

The magazine said Ford was asked about N.C. State turning in Clemson.

"I don't know if he did it or not. If he did, that's his business. And if we turn them in, it's our business."

Kiffin: "I didn't turn him in. But if I had, I wouldn't have been wrong."

After an open date, the Tigers returned home for a Top Twenty matchup against North Carolina. Clemson broke out the orange pants and held on for a 16-13 win after Tar Heels coach Dick Crum opted against a game-tying field goal with less than a minute left.

On fourth-and-four from Clemson's fifteen, North Carolina tailback Tyrone Anthony dropped a pass in the flat that would have given the Tar Heels a first down and possibly a touchdown. Ford, whose team improved to 6-1-1, was happy with the win but frustrated with poor tackling and overall inconsistency.

The big news Sunday morning had nothing to do with the victory that moved the Tigers a step closer to another ACC title. Dan Foster of the *Greenville News* reported that Clemson was likely headed to a bowl in 1982, despite the NCAA's investigation. NCAA policy dictated that a team could attend a bowl if it accepted a bid before being notified of probation against a bowl appearance, and Foster reported the NCAA's penalties would not come down before bid day on November 20.

Two days later, the *Greenville News* reversed course with a 1A story topped with this headline: "Clemson recruiting penalty report may be near." Foster wrote that there was a "great likelihood" penalties from the NCAA and ACC would be presented to Clemson before November 20.

To this point, it had not been publicly known that the ACC would impose its own penalties independent of the NCAA's punishment. The *Washington Post* reported that the ACC voted to place Clemson on probation for two years with penalties including loss of television revenue for that period.

Clemson's hearing with the NCAA's Committee on Infractions had unfolded in secrecy during the Tigers' open date following the win in Raleigh. School officials participated in three days of hearings with the six-member committee in a Chicago suburb. Foster wrote that the news of the ACC's punitive measures "came like a thunderbolt to outsiders who have followed Clemson's investigation by the NCAA."

"The public could not have been quite prepared for the fact that it would be the Atlantic Coast Conference which would hold the decisive hand on whether Clemson goes to a bowl this year or not...In fact, some of the people most angered by what they believe Clemson has done are the members of its own conference. They have to compete against Clemson, and they have the most to lose, head-to-head, by whatever has helped an opponent. If they believe it's illegal help, that worsens their mood."

Cindy Powell, editor in chief of the *Tiger*, wrote on November 11: "It's time for this probation thing to end. The rumors and the speculation have gone on too long and Clemson University's reputation has suffered too much. No national championship is worth this."

The number eleven Tigers were preparing for a trip to Maryland, a game that contained major ACC title implications. Both teams were 4-0 in the conference, and North Carolina had been knocked out of the race with losses to the Tigers and Terps. The distractions were frustrating to Ford.

Before a regional CBS television audience, Clemson went up 24-7 in College Park before fending off a late rally by Maryland quarterback Boomer Esiason and winning 24-22. The Terps were in field-goal range late when safety Terry Kinard forced a fumble that was recovered by Reggie Pleasant. Maryland's final hope was extinguished when Billy Davis snared an interception with thirty-seven seconds left.

The Tigers' final conference game would take place in two weeks against Wake Forest in Tokyo, but Ford's team essentially wrapped up its second consecutive conference title with the win over Maryland. The

Tigers had won seven consecutive games since the 0-1-1 start and were in contention for another trip to the Orange Bowl.

Three days after the victory in College Park, as the team prepared for a home clash with rival South Carolina, Atchley announced that Clemson would not attend a bowl game. He also announced his plan for a reorganization of the athletics department and said details would come the next week. Atchley later said he preferred to wait until after the rivalry game to announce the bowl news, but media outlets were on top of the story and reporting that bowls were removing Clemson from consideration. Ford notified his team of the news at 3:00 p.m. on Tuesday, an hour before Atchley's announcement and four days before the visit from the Gamecocks.

The penalties had yet to be announced, but the *Greenville News* was reporting that Clemson would incur two years of probation from the NCAA and three from the ACC. Foster criticized the conference's punishment and said it could create major strife between Clemson and the ACC.

"The NCAA, which has handled hundreds of probation cases, looked at the same evidence and came up with something less. But that has happened before, and other conferences have reconsidered, if not immediately then later. That seems a clear possibility in this case unless the hostility is so great that the relationships break down completely."

In the *Tiger*, Homer Jordan reacted to the news that the team would be home for the holidays: "We were getting ready to go to another major bowl, hopefully the Orange Bowl again. It was as if a Mack truck backed over us or something."

The rivalry game was overshadowed by the news of the ACC doing the unprecedented and imposing its own probation, but Ford managed to stay on message as he fretted about facing the 4-6 Gamecocks.

Ford, whose team was favored by three touchdowns, said he anticipated "one of those too-close-for-comfort affairs" against South Carolina. The number ten Tigers had been lucky to win their previous two games over Maryland and North Carolina by a total of five points.

"We can't stand prosperity," Ford said at his Tuesday press luncheon. "We love to have friends. We love to give the ball back, and we can't cut nobody off. We can't dominate nobody. The thing I don't like about our team is we don't dominate. We don't have that mean streak. They'll let you off the ground so you can get ahead. I don't think we can live on luck anymore. We're lucked out. So we'd better start making things happen."

The Tigers produced the desired domination in a 24-6 ripping of the Gamecocks for their eighth consecutive victory. After the game, Ford said he spent far too little time with his team in the days leading up to it: "I don't see how they did it, not with the injuries, and the information of the past week, and other things."

Ford still had not publicly discussed probation, but he gave his take on the state of the program after the Tigers improved to 8-1-1.

"I think we'll have a good year recruiting. Our football field hasn't changed a bit. Our buildings aren't going to fall down. Our crowd hasn't changed. We're going full speed ahead to have an outstanding football program...I know it's hard to win year in and year out, but nothing is harder than this year."

Two days after the win over South Carolina, the NCAA news came down. Citing more than 150 individual rule violations dating as far back as the 1976–77 academic year, the NCAA docked Clemson twenty scholarships over two years in addition to the ban on bowls and live television. Two assistant coaches were placed on probation that froze their salaries and restricted them from various forms of recruiting. Four unidentified university boosters were barred from taking part in recruiting activities for at least two years.

The scholarship penalties were regarded as the most severe punishment ever handed down by the NCAA. Clemson had a fifteen-day period to appeal the NCAA sanctions but chose not to do so. At a press conference, Atchley shot down rumors that Ford would resign.

Clemson's administration was furious with the ACC, whose faculty athletics representatives voted for the extra year of probation without conducting their own investigation. Clemson was hoping the ACC would grant the appeal and allow the Tigers to play in a bowl game in 1984. The ACC had never barred a team from going to a bowl in its thirty-year existence.

Atchley said at the press conference:

> We have appealed the ACC decision, but so far we've come home
> empty-handed. Why did the ACC decide to impose such a severe
> penalty on the same facts as the NCAA? I frankly don't have an
> explanation and can only refer you to them for comment. I will say
> I know the ACC made their decision without benefit of the complete
> picture. I just don't think they are aware, or we didn't make it clear,
> of the innovations and positive steps we have taken and plan to take
> to correct our problems...We were never under investigation by the
> ACC. We were by the NCAA. The ACC had no material but what
> we supplied them. They didn't really give a good explanation [for
> the penalties].

The day after the probation news became official, Ford and the football
team were in Atlanta for their flight to Tokyo. Ford told UPI it was "a
relief" to hear the penalties after the nineteen-month investigation.

Ford relaxes and reads the newspaper on a charter flight. *Courtesy of Clemson University Sports
Information Department.*

"A lot of times the unknown is worse than the known. I heard some things today and read some things that made things that happened sound worse than they were." Asked if some of the infractions had been distorted, Ford said: "Amazingly so."

Freshman running back Terrence Flagler told UPI that the NCAA investigation was "sort of like a curtain over us all year."

"Even when we had a big win, it would always come up. We were never able to enjoy a victory. There were more questions about probation, it seemed, than how the team won the game."

Herman Helms of the *State* wrote that the NCAA's measures against Clemson revealed "a corrupt operation that is an embarrassment not only to one of South Carolina's leading institutions of higher learning but to intercollegiate athletics in general."

"The distasteful report prompts a major question: If this is the way national championships are won, do they have any real meaning?"

A 1981 study revealed that forty-two of sixty-two members of major football conferences had been caught cheating. Dave Kindred of the *Washington Post* assailed Clemson in a column that ran on Thanksgiving Day, writing that probation would hurt Clemson's recruiting to such an extent that the program "will suffer for a decade."

Follow the orange Tiger paws on the roads outside Clemson, S.C., and they lead to tall piles of cash. The NCAA said there was cash for signing up with the school, cash for cars, cash for clothes, cash for TV sets, cash for being 'Specialty Teams Player of the Week,' cash for phone calls and dental bills and airline trips. The head coach, Danny Ford, promised a prospect he'd find a job for the boy's mother. Someone promised scholarships to a prospect's two sisters.

These violations strike at the heart of the NCAA idea that college athletics is an amateur enterprise that is part of the educational process. These are violations that occur only with approval from the highest levels of an athletic program—approval by conscious assent, or approval by a convenient turn of the head.

Fully 15 violations dealt with the use of automobiles, suggesting that the NCAA's punishments ought to include revocation of driver's licenses.

Newsweek also got in a dig: "Considering that 15 of the 150 violations involved free cars and free rides, Clemson's main consolation is that nobody got ticketed for reckless driving."

The Tigers were wearing their orange pants when they emerged in front of eighty thousand fans in Tokyo to take on Wake Forest. Clemson expected to trounce the Deacons in a fashion similar to its 82-24 thrashing in 1981, but Ford and his team considered themselves lucky to win 21-17 after being outgained 461-286.

Clemson finished the season ranked number eight by the Associated Press. The UPI coaches' poll dropped the Tigers out of its Top Twenty because of a longstanding policy to exclude teams on probation.

Former Clemson signees Terry Minor and James Cofer, whose allegations of recruiting violations in late 1980 triggered the NCAA's investigation, ended up signing with Louisiana Tech but dropped out and transferred to Division II Carson Newman. In the summer of 1982, a Tennessee judge threw out their $12 million lawsuit against Clemson, Ford and others involved in their recruitment.

Cofer told the *Tiger* that Clemson's penalties were too light.

"I figure Clemson got what it had coming. But Clemson can always bounce back. Two years, that goes too fast. After two years, Clemson can start all over again. It's too late for me to start over."

Chapter 6

1983

When the calendar turned to 1983, Clemson people were finding it hard to move past the rage from events of late 1982.

The Tigers won nine games during the regular season, claimed a conference title and were ranked in the Top Ten. Yet there was no trip to the Orange Bowl, Cotton Bowl or any bowl. The ACC had stepped in and imposed probation on its own to ensure Clemson would face immediate and severe punishment for recruiting violations.

Players blasted the ACC to the *Tiger*, Clemson's student newspaper.

Running back Stacey Driver: "I feel like it was the only way that the other schools could get to us. I know that no one in the conference can beat us."

Defensive lineman William Devane: "Being a player, I think that we pay the bills of the other people. I mean, we'll be the ones sitting at home watching the bowl games on TV."

Running back Kenny Flowers: "I don't think that we did anything that any other major school hasn't done. We're such a small school, and we won the national championship. I guess they were just jealous."

By January, it was becoming evident that a major rift was developing between university president Bill Atchley and athletics director Bill McLellan. One of Atchley's primary responses to probation was announcing a plan to change McLellan's responsibilities and put associate athletics director Bobby Robinson in charge of the football and basketball programs, recruiting rules monitoring and budgeting. McLellan's new responsibilities would be business affairs and marketing.

Atchley also planned to create a position above McLellan in the athletics department, someone who would oversee the athletics director and report directly to the president.

McLellan, a former Clemson football player who rose through the ranks before becoming athletics director in 1971 and overseeing a period of tremendous growth and innovation in Clemson athletics, thumbed his nose at the planned restructuring. He told the *Greenville News* that he was taking a "wait and see" attitude toward the idea. He said he'd address it "when the time comes and if that becomes a problem."

A number of trustees were aligned with McLellan and also opposed Atchley's plans. The board's executive committee instructed Atchley to avoid commenting publicly on NCAA probation and the proposed reorganization. Only later was it revealed that Atchley barely survived an attempt by the board to oust him during this period in January 1983. His idea to create a position over McLellan was dropped two months later.

Clemson's academic community was showing its disgust toward the athletics department. The faculty senate voted to support Atchley's reorganization plan and called for McLellan's dismissal. Another proposal said faculty would disassociate itself from the athletics department if "satisfactory changes are not made to put the athletic house in order within a reasonable time."

Faculty senator Robert Taylor, of the College of Sciences, said the problems under McLellan were "of long standing," referring to major violations under former basketball coach Tates Locke in the 1970s.

"The only thing in common between the two probations is the athletic director. The tone of the department is set by the athletic director and the responsibility of the department is upon the director ultimately. I think the dismissal of Mr. McLellan is more important than Phase I, Phase II or ay other phases that might be offered in the future."

McLellan wrote to IPTAY members urging Clemson supporters to "come together and show what we are made of."

We have had a long, hard, trying time—full of bad publicity that has been too widely aired. Nevertheless, let's start off by remembering that behind every problem there is likely to be a blessing. Wounds can heal and the body be stronger than ever before. Many of you have called with suggestions about what we should do with our athletic program. We appreciate your concern and help…Clemson is a leader, not a quitter. We have to pick ourselves up and go on to better things.

The NCAA and, especially, the ACC findings seem harsh, but we must realize that we did, in fact, commit errors which were in violation of the athletic rules under which our program operates. So now we have to take our medicine—no matter how bitter it may taste.

Clemson's football program, our other athletic programs, and especially our fans are the envy of all our opponents. They can't understand why our IPTAY program is the largest in the world. Most of them have more graduates than we do, and are located in far more populous areas. Still, even though we are tucked away in the corner of a small state, we have managed to have sixty-three thousand fans at our home football games, while thousands follow us on the road and to bowls.

McLellan got creative in finding a way around the NCAA's ban on live television, arranging for games to be shown on a tape-delay basis by ESPN and USA Network. Clemson would play before an expanded Memorial Stadium in 1983 with an upper deck atop the north stands. The expansion added fifteen thousand new seats to Death Valley, and the Tigers had a seven-game home schedule.

The continuing momentum of a probation-strapped program bothered some people in the ACC. A newspaper writer in Virginia derisively wrote that the stadium expansion and TV improvisations presented proof that Clemson was rebelling against the penalties and the rest of the conference.

Clemson was also building a new 4,160-foot home for Danny Ford, who was entering his fifth full season as head coach of the Tigers. The IPTAY board of directors voted to finance the home after the Tigers claimed the 1981 national title, and McLellan responded to criticism of the arrangement by saying Clemson was simply remaining competitive with other major schools who'd done the same thing for their head coaches. The home ended up exceeding the budget and costing more than $500,000.

Ford suffered a great loss in January 1983 when Bear Bryant had a massive heart attack and died at the age of sixty-nine. Just weeks earlier,

Bryant announced his retirement after a victory over Illinois in the Liberty Bowl. Ford played and coached for Bryant before taking a job at Virginia Tech in 1974. He was visiting a recruit in North Carolina when he learned of Bryant's passing.

In mid-July, the ACC issued a news release concerning its upcoming preseason media poll.

"The Tigers aren't eligible for the title this year, and under terms of Clemson's probation no games against the Tigers will be counted in the league standings."

To this point, Clemson was aware only that it was not eligible for the ACC title in 1983 and 1984. Kerry Capps, a writer for the *Orange and White*, wrote that this revelation robbed Clemson of the motivation to play the role of spoiler in the ACC. It was interpreted as a slap in the face.

"The latest news from the ACC only solidifies the feeling common among Clemson people that an injustice has been committed," Capps wrote.

Clemson was not ranked in the 1983 preseason Associated Press poll despite finishing number eight in 1982. The Tigers had amassed a 21-1-1 record over the previous two seasons and had won twelve consecutive ACC games.

Ford, whose record stood at 36-10-1 entering 1983, gave benign observations when he publicly discussed the upcoming season. He said that "time is the biggest healer" and announced he wanted to treat every home game like a bowl game.

Privately, it was a different story. Ford and his team were galvanized by an all-consuming hunger to show no mercy to a conference that stuck it to the football program the previous November. In an August interview with the *Orange and White*, Ford was asked how much motivation his team would draw from the ACC's decision not to count Clemson's conference games.

"If our guys go out there and compete against another school, one school is going to win. They don't have to count it. But if those guys don't believe they've been hit or hit at, then they didn't see the ballgame. If we're Clemson and we hit people like we're supposed to, they'll know."

Ford crouches and watches warm-ups for a game at Death Valley, a venue that became known as one of the most difficult in college football during his tenure. *Courtesy of Clemson University Sports Information Department.*

Clemson lost some headliners from the 1982 team, including quarterback Homer Jordan, all-American safety Terry Kinard and defensive end Andy Headen. The offense was moving to more drop-back passing to suit the talents of junior quarterback Mike Eppley, who gained valuable experience in 1982 with Jordan struggling with a knee injury. The Tigers boasted perhaps the best defensive line in the country thanks largely to the interior tandem of Devane and junior William Perry, who combined for ninety-seven tackles and seven sacks in 1982.

The 1982 team sputtered at the start, losing at Georgia and suffering a tie at home against Boston College. Ford was concerned about another slow start in 1983, and after an easy win over Western Carolina in the opener, his fears were realized when Clemson went to Boston College and suffered a 31-16 whipping.

The Tigers led 13-3 at the half and 16-10 after three quarters, but quarterback Doug Flutie abused Clemson's defense for three fourth-quarter touchdowns. A year earlier, Flutie drove the Tigers' defensive line crazy by escaping containment for big gains. This time, he completed twenty of twenty-six passes for 223 yards and two touchdowns. Running back Troy Stradford gashed the Tigers on the ground with 179 yards and a touchdown on twenty-three rushes.

Ford was exasperated by five fumbles, three of them lost, and an interception. One of the fumbles was by running back Stacey Driver at Clemson's eleven-yard line in the fourth quarter. Boston College went on to finish 9-3 and ranked in the Top Twenty.

"We certainly didn't have to come this far to get beat this bad," Ford told reporters after the game. "I didn't do a good job of coaching, because when you have someone down 16-3 this shouldn't happen."

Georgia was visiting a week later, and on Sunday, Ford told his coaches and players to skip watching the Boston College film. He vowed that the defeat wouldn't be talked about again in 1983.

Ford said the Tigers were "only an average football team," and that's the main reason he vetoed a request from his players to wear the sacred orange pants against Georgia. His team wasn't playing physically enough on offense and wasn't tackling well enough on defense for him to sign off on the special garb.

"We aren't going to use them until we look like a Clemson team," Ford said at his Tuesday press luncheon. "The super powers will not be with us this week. We've got to earn this on our own."

Clemson was up 10 on Georgia after three quarters but couldn't close the deal. The game ended in a 16-16 tie after Kevin Butler hit a thirty-one-yard field goal with thirty-eight seconds left. A sixty-eight-yard field goal try by Donald Igwebuike was just short. Then Georgia had a shot to win, but a sixty-six-yard try from Butler was also short.

Tim Ellerbe, columnist for the Anderson *Independent-Mail*, described the surreal scene after the game: "Saturday evening, 75,000 Clemson fans and 6,000 Georgia followers left Clemson Memorial Stadium not knowing how to act. Georgia fans wanted to cuss Clemson fans. Clemson fans wanted to cuss Georgia fans. And nobody could come up with anything good (or bad) to say. So they all stood around and got drunk."

Clemson fans probably felt worse because their team dominated the line of scrimmage in the second and third quarters. The Tigers held the

Bulldogs to 130 rushing yards, and the defensive line caused Georgia running backs to fumble twice. It was precisely the performance Ford was looking for, except the result. Terry Hoage, Georgia's all-American safety, blocked two field-goal attempts by Bob Paulling—including a 32-yard try that would have put Clemson up 19-6 with 2:32 left in the third quarter.

Seven days later, Clemson ran down the Hill wearing orange pants, and many people wondered why. The Tigers' foe that day, Georgia Tech, was 0-2 and a three-touchdown underdog in its first year of ACC competition—far from a stature that typically merited the prized britches.

The Yellow Jackets, who'd lost to Furman a week earlier, had the unenviable distinction as the first ACC opponent of the Tigers' probation sentence. To Ford and his team, it was a big game and a symbolic game because there was hell to pay.

Clemson dismembered its visitors 41-14, moving the Tigers' ACC winning streak to thirteen games, even though the result didn't count officially as a result of the conference's punishment.

"We've got to go onto the field against ACC teams with bad feelings," quarterback Mike Eppley told reporters. "We think we owe a lot of conference teams something. Nothing dirty. But good, clean nastiness."

Kenny Flowers and Stacey Driver combined for 195 rushing yards, and Eppley completed eleven of eighteen passes for 129 yards and a touchdown. The emphasis on passing was a result of Ford opening things up after limited passing against Boston College and Georgia. Clemson outgained the Yellow Jackets 355-111.

The Tigers had an open date to prepare for a visit from Virginia, a team they beat 48-0 a year earlier in Charlottesville. The 4-1 Cavaliers were off to their best start in thirty years but walked away from Death Valley on the wrong end of a 41-24 score.

Ford wasn't happy after the game because Clemson failed to put Virginia away. The Cavaliers, led by quarterback Don Majkowski, totaled 414 yards.

Alan Cannon, sports editor for the *Tiger*, wasn't impressed. He published a mock classified ad the next week that read: "WANTED: Football players to fill out Division I team. Must have talent, physical capabilities, and desire. High school experience necessary. MUST DISPLAY KILLER INSTINCT. No Clemson players need apply."

A week later at Duke, the Tigers couldn't put the Blue Devils away after taking a 24-3 lead late in the first half. Duke was 0-5 coming in, but Clemson needed a late pass deflection to win 38-31 after the Devils reached the Tigers' eleven-yard line with a minute left. Quarterback Ben Bennett torched the Tigers' secondary by throwing for 367 yards and four touchdowns while completing thirty-four of fifty-three passes.

A day after the narrow victory, Ford met with ACC officials in Charlotte to vent about officiating. The Tigers totaled eighteen penalties for 134 yards against Duke, and the Blue Devils had four for 45 yards. Eight of Clemson's penalties were for defensive offsides, a result of Duke changing its snap count.

Ford's explanation for the Sunday meeting: "Enough's enough."

"We are getting held a tremendous number of times," he said at his Tuesday press conference. "I'm very concerned about the holding, especially when I go back and see on the film that I'm right. It's a total disadvantage to our youngsters who are trying to be successful on each play. The rules were supposed to make things equal, not give one side an advantage."

Ford and longtime assistant Woody McCorvey (both crouching) watch the action from the sidelines of Death Valley. *Courtesy of Clemson University Sports Information Department.*

A reporter asked Ford if he believed Clemson was a marked team in the ACC. The coach grinned and didn't respond.

Clemson beat N.C. State 27-17 in its next game, but the final score didn't reveal how much the Tigers struggled to win in front of their home fans. The Wolfpack, which ended up finishing 3-8, went up 17-9 on its first possession of the second half before Clemson rallied.

Late in the third quarter, Eppley scored on a twenty-eight-yard run and a successful two-point conversion tied the score at seventeen. N.C. State drove into Clemson territory on the next drive, but Rod McSwain snared an interception at the twenty-five to snuff out the threat. On the next play, Eppley hit Ray Williams for a seventy-five-yard touchdown that put the Tigers up seven.

The Tigers had to sweat out another victory the next week against Wake Forest, holding on for a 24-17 win after the Deacons botched several scoring opportunities deep in Clemson territory. The game drew just sixty-six thousand fans to Death Valley, far short of the expanded stadium's capacity.

Chris Smith, Clemson beat writer for the *Greenville News*, wrote that it was "just another typical Saturday afternoon for the Clemson Tigers and their Houdini season of escapes. For it seems the more the Tigers win, the uglier they get. And one has to wonder just how much longer they can simultaneously beat themselves and their opponents."

The Tigers improved to 6-1-1 and extended their home unbeaten streak to nineteen games while improving their ACC winning streak to seventeen games. But struggling to beat Duke, N.C. State and Wake Forest—teams that would combine for a 10-23 record in 1983—was not a heartening trend with difficult games remaining against North Carolina, Maryland and South Carolina.

Clemson was a seven-point underdog heading to Chapel Hill. The Tar Heels were ranked number three nationally before they suffered a 28-26 loss at Maryland on the same day as Clemson's victory over Wake Forest.

The Tigers' rivalry with North Carolina, already heated in large part because both programs had been powerful for several years, was elevated to a nastier level as a result of the ACC's imposition of probation and the belief that the Tar Heels helped lead the charge to bring Clemson to its knees.

Earlier in the year, in an interview with the *Daily News* of Philadelphia, Tar Heels coach Dick Crum was asked how much Clemson's 1981 national title helped the ACC's football image.

"I think it helped in one way, the fact that they won it. But I think it hurt because they were put on probation. Obviously, they bought it. I don't think the other schools in the league want to be put in that class."

Ford was asked about Crum's quote the week of the game.

"He can say what he wants to, but I think he needs to know a little bit more about the history of that. I think if you've got something to say to somebody, it's better to say it to their faces, not to newspapers."

Clemson's players already viewed North Carolina with disdain. Crum's words fueled the fire, and the Tigers administered a 16-3 whipping that sent a resounding, defiant message to the Tar Heels and the rest of the ACC.

A week after playing what Ford described as their worst game of the season, the Tigers served up their best in holding North Carolina to its lowest point total since 1978. Clemson had not lost in Chapel Hill since 1971, inspiring a fan to fashion a sign that read: "Clemson Tigers, King of the Heel."

It was the Tigers' turn to talk after the game. Ford exchanged bitter words with Crum during a brief meeting at midfield. An estimated six thousand Clemson fans in attendance chanted "ACC! ACC! ACC!" some of them holding up middle fingers instead of index fingers.

William Perry, helmet in hand, walked off the field with a grin and said, "We own this place." Perry later told reporters that the Tigers didn't want to just beat the Tar Heels. "We wanted to beat them bad and rub it in."

Several Tigers, including defensive tackle Ray Brown, sang "We work hard for the money," taunting the North Carolina fan contingent that remained as they strutted off the field.

Defensive back Tim Childers told the *Orange and White*:

> *I can't believe that he said it. Coach Crum said we were a disgrace. I don't know why he said it. It sure didn't help his team any...If [Crum] wants a national championship so bad, why don't he go buy him one if that's all it takes? Clemson didn't buy a championship. They*

just got us on a bunch of little picky violations. What it all comes down to is that we've got a national championship ring and he doesn't.

Ford said his players hadn't enjoyed winning this much "in a long, long time." Asked about Crum's comments in his postgame press conference, he responded, "One thing you have to remember is that you never give your opponent something to read about. It's like a Chihuahua: Your mouth can overload your rear end and get you in trouble."

North Carolina's players were taken aback by the Tigers' behavior during the game. Receiver Mark Smith to the *Orange and White:* "I don't know how to say it. It's not that I think Clemson plays dirty on the field. But it's the attitude they have. It's the distasteful way they behave towards other teams." Tar Heels offensive tackle Joe Conwell: "We don't motivate on any hate factor. Our motivation is our goals. If Clemson does hate us as a winning edge, that's a shame. That's not good for intercollegiate football. And if that's what it is, it makes the loss easier to accept."

The friction between the two teams overshadowed a stifling showing by a Clemson defense that had been startlingly average for much of the season. North Carolina quarterback Scott Stankavage called it "the best defensive football team I've ever played against." The Tar Heels drove inside Clemson's thirty-five-yard line six times but got nothing five times in large part because of the Tigers' overwhelming superiority on the defensive line.

Randy Coleman, columnist for the Anderson *Independent-Mail,* noticed Clemson fans' mushrooming hatred of the ACC. It was a sharp contrast from just two years earlier, when backers took pride in bringing recognition to the conference during the 1981 national title season.

"Saturday the cheer had a different ring to it," Coleman wrote. "Clemson fans took a vengeful delight in shouting, not about the conference, but at it."

Winners of six consecutive games and ranked for the first time all season at number seventeen, Ford's team had more business to tend to in its last home game of 1983. Number eleven Maryland was coming to town with a chance to win the official ACC title, and the Tigers were interested in having their say.

Ford spent the week fretting about quarterback Boomer Esiason, who'd given the Tigers fits the previous year. A week earlier, Maryland had gone to Auburn and lost 35-23. Led by all-American running back Bo Jackson, Auburn finished the season 11-1 and ranked number three after defeating four Top Ten opponents in its last five games.

The stadium was in a festive mood thanks in part to the release of an estimated 315,000 balloons before the game. The announced crowd of 81,000 was deafening from the start, and the noise only increased as Clemson poured it on in a 52-27 annihilation. In handing Maryland its worst defeat since 1971, the Tigers roared to a 28-7 halftime advantage and ended up with 351 rushing yards. The crowd noise cost Clemson two timeouts, and Kerry Capps of the *Orange and White* wrote: "For the first time in what seems like ages, fan noise was actually a problem."

In the final minutes, a final score from elsewhere blared over the PA system: Virginia 17, North Carolina 14. The team getting flattened on the Death Valley turf had become the official ACC champion, and everyone in orange took savage delight in embarrassing the supposed kings of the conference.

Coleman's column on Sunday read: "In the minds of the entire Clemson football team, Maryland had to earn its title. A Clemson victory and a Maryland defeat would give the unofficial title to the Tigers. And that unofficial title was priceless. The contest was a mismatch. Maryland played the role of Atlanta. Clemson was Sherman."

Fans ripped down the goal posts in the east end zone to celebrate their team's third consecutive undefeated season in conference play. Since a loss at Maryland way back in 1980, the Tigers had amassed a 19-0 mark in the ACC.

In the locker room afterward, the players modified a chant they'd yelled after victories for years. Rather than shout: "We don't give a damn about the whole state of (defeated opponent) because we're from Clemson U!" after this victory, they screamed: "We don't give a damn about the whole ACC because we're from Clemson U!"

"It doesn't really matter what a group of men somewhere says," Tigers offensive lineman Andy Cheatham told reporters afterward. "It's different on the football field. We are the ACC champions. We're 7-0."

Said senior defensive tackle James Robinson: "Oh yeah, we're very much the ACC champs. And I'm sure everyone else in the league will say it, too. If a man whips me, I know he's the winner."

Maryland coach Bobby Ross said afterward that he knew the Tigers would be tough defensively, but he was surprised with how swiftly they moved the ball on offense. They overpowered the Terps on the ground with 351 rushing yards, led by Kevin Mack's 186 yards and three touchdowns on thirty carries. Eppley passed for 194 yards and three touchdowns. Clemson improved to 10-0 while wearing orange pants.

Media in Maryland's locker room happened upon a demoralized Esiason.

"Looks like we're really excited in here, doesn't it?" the quarterback said. "We won the thing today and didn't do a damned thing. It's the worst loss of my entire life. And I mean even back to little league football."

Esiason said Maryland was "still the honest ACC champs." But he admitted it was a hollow achievement given the Terps' feeble resistance against a superior team.

"They beat all the teams, and they're a member of the ACC whether anybody likes it or not," he said. "One thing I know is that they're the best team we've played all year, including Auburn."

In a span of one week, Clemson completely transformed its season by pillaging bitter rivals. Ford commended his team after the game.

"Whether you like it or not, you've got to say they went out against the best in the conference and won. That's something nobody else did, isn't it?"

Ford and his team couldn't celebrate long. Their final game was in Columbia against South Carolina, a team led by a galvanizing first-year coach named Joe Morrison. At 5-5 the Gamecocks had exceeded expectations, and Ford was concerned about facing their split-back veer option offense. He told reporters it was "the best football team at South Carolina in a long time."

Early in the week, rumors circulated that Ford might replace Jerry Stovall at LSU. His name was mentioned in articles by the Atlanta *Constitution* and Florida *Times-Union*, but Ford said there was nothing to it.

The Gamecocks warmed up at Williams-Brice Stadium in all garnet uniforms but emerged in all black just before kickoff. Morrison, who'd already made a name for his own all-black wardrobe, had said little to discourage rumors during the week that his team would wear the color from head to toe against the Tigers.

Clemson went up 9-0 early but considered itself fortunate to enter halftime up 12-10. The Gamecocks drove seventy-one yards to the Clemson nine before two sacks made them settle for a field goal that made the score 9-3. After the Tigers kicked a field goal, South Carolina drove eighty yards in eight plays for a touchdown to trim it to 12-10. A blocked field goal by Rod McSwain kept the Gamecocks from going into halftime with a lead.

The Tigers created breathing room by scoring on their first two possessions of the third quarter, taking a 22-10 lead. The Gamecocks made it 22-13 with a field goal and then drove inside Clemson's ten, but Allen Mitchell threw an interception to extinguish the Gamecocks' hopes of an upset. The Tigers had won four straight over the Gamecocks for the first time in forty-three years.

Defensive lineman Ray Brown recovered a fumble on the Gamecocks' final possession and held the ball over his head as he looked toward enemy fans behind Clemson's bench who had taunted him all game. A few of the fans held up handfuls of cash, and Brown responded: "Give me the money! I need all I can get!"

Clemson's rivalries with Georgia, North Carolina and Maryland had become heated in recent years, but the Tigers still took great delight in beating their in-state foes. All year long, they'd seen stickers on the bumpers of cars driven by Gamecocks fans: "CLEMSON—THE BEST TEAM MONEY CAN BUY."

Brown told reporters after the game: "If you wear black, you're usually going to a funeral. I guess we buried the dead. Anyway, good guys always wear white."

The game was marred by a benches-clearing brawl in the last minute, and both coaches lamented the fracas.

"This rivalry is getting more and more intense, especially from their part," Ford told the media that day. "Losing the last few years may have a lot to do with that. I don't think our people had any great intensity before they came out on the field today. But I know that our people are not going to be able to come in here and be a normal football team and expect to be successful anymore."

Soon thereafter, Ford would be named ACC coach of the year by the Associated Press. Before he boarded a bus for the trip back to

Clemson, Ford said that day in Columbia that he'd never been so tired after a season.

But he'd seldom been prouder, either.

"I'm just so damn happy they're 9-1-1, I can't hardly stand it. I want to go eat. I want to go hug them and love them and cry with them and just congratulate them for doing such a great job, and I just want to quit for two days. I don't want to do nothing, I'm telling you."

Chapter 7
1984

Animosity toward the ACC was still boiling hot among Clemson supporters as they moved into 1984 after going a second consecutive season without a bowl appearance.

Clemson's administration still believed there was legitimate hope of the ACC softening its three-year probation and allowing for a bowl trip after the 1984 season. The NCAA's sanctions began in November of 1982 and ended with the last regular-season game of 1984. Clemson supporters still couldn't understand why the ACC's penalties, handed down after zero investigation on the conference's part, were more punitive than the NCAA's.

Some supporters called for Clemson to follow Southern California's lead and ignore NCAA and conference sanctions. The Trojans were hammered with bans on bowls and TV coverage in 1982 and 1983 after a football coach was accused of ticket scalping.

Athletics director Bill McLellan worked behind the scenes to cultivate support from other ACC schools. In a letter dated February 17, 1984, McLellan wrote Duke athletics director Tom Butters asking for a "personal evaluation" of Clemson's punishment by the ACC. McLellan wrote that Clemson had made a "total effort" to comply with the rules, and he noted that none of the players or coaches involved in the NCAA violations were still with the program by this point.

"Having worked with me through the years, I believe you know that I acknowledge errors made and don't ask for special favors," McLellan wrote to Butters. "I have not attempted to avoid the penalties imposed in this situation and I have exerted every effort to assure that we have taken corrective measures wherever we have control. I feel the impact of the penalties has been significant on our program and we can accept that."

McLellan wrote that president Bill Atchley and the Board of Trustees were anxious to know where the ACC stood on a possible appeal. Clemson had the impression that the conference would be receptive to an appeal, prompting hopes that the Tigers would play in a bowl in 1984.

At the ACC spring meetings in May, McLellan voted with the majority on two baseball-related decisions and angered Tigers coach Bill Wilhelm in the process. The conference's baseball coaches voted to recommend changing the dates and location of the ACC tournament, and the athletics directors voted down both proposals. In the *Orange and White*, Wilhelm called the decision "asinine."

"The ACC took a giant step backwards…The athletic directors, in their limited wisdom, said to hell with the game, the players and the fans and voted for an April tournament."

It was speculated that McLellan sought solidarity with his ACC counterparts on this matter in hopes of generating goodwill for an appeal of football probation. Some people even believed a behind-the-scenes deal was in the works between Clemson and the ACC.

As Clemson supporters pondered the thought of a third consecutive season without a bowl appearance, some called for the school to leave the ACC if the conference denied the appeal. Clemson didn't strongly consider it, in part because of a recent Supreme Court decision that allowed schools and conferences to negotiate their own television packages.

Clemson requested a meeting with ACC officials to appeal the extra year of probation, and the opportunity came late on the night of June 28 in Chicago. The appeal was soundly rejected when five of seven ACC faculty athletics representatives voted against it. Clemson needed five votes for the appeal to go through, but only Maryland and Wake Forest provided support.

Atchley released a statement that said Clemson was "extremely disappointed" with the rejection.

Clemson University is an active and viable member of the Atlantic Coast Conference, and we intend to remain that way. However we do not agree with the decision. We have felt from the beginning that the sanctions handed down from the NCAA were severe but fair. The additional sanctions handed down from the conference were, in our opinion, not appropriate. We also feel that the constitution of the conference regarding such matters was not followed.

In late July, Kerry Capps of the *Orange and White* captured the mood of Clemson people: "Clemson supporters are, once again, angry and defiant. There seems to be a consensus of opinion among Tiger supporters that Clemson is big enough to live without the ACC. Talk of withdrawing from the conference altogether, or—at least—defying the ACC's bowl order in 1984, is widespread."

Danny Ford, preparing for his sixth season running the football program, didn't try to hide his disgust. During a preseason ACC media gathering at Pinehurst Resort in North Carolina, he ripped the ACC for failing to abide by its own constitution as it addressed Clemson's appeal.

"I don't think they handled it well," he told reporters. "They didn't follow the rules. I wasn't very impressed with them…They made up the rules as they went along on how they were going to treat Clemson."

Clemson believed the ACC erred in allowing its faculty athletics representatives to act as the conference's enforcement body. Clemson also objected to the faculty athletics representatives voting on the appeal given that they initially decided on the punishment that was being appealed.

"The conference's words were they'd help us with the NCAA," Ford said at Pinehurst. "They helped us, all right. I'm still trying to figure out what we can and can't do. There are a couple of close friends we got votes from, but we're used to that. If we want to be in this conference, we'll do what they say because of the 18 other sports."

The *Greenville News* didn't approve of Ford's reaction, running an editorial that said the coach was using a "redneck mentality." The paper urged Ford to "show more class" and said his "whining" produced similar behavior from his players and fans.

Clemson fans were furious. Five days later, two full pages of letters to the editor ran in the *Greenville News* as fans blasted the newspaper and voiced staunch support for Ford. A correction from the newspaper accompanied the letters, offering an apology for "wrong word choice."

After closing the 1983 season with convincing wins over North Carolina, Maryland and South Carolina to finish 9-1-1, Clemson was regarded as a powerhouse in 1984. The Tigers had amassed a 30-2-2 record over the previous three seasons and returned almost everyone on offense, including star quarterback Mike Eppley. Some preseason polls had the Tigers ranked number one. Almost all of them had the Tigers in the Top Ten.

Probation was still a hot topic and a galvanizing theme as the season approached. Players wore shirts that read: "On probation and still kickin' ass." When ACC writers made an August stop in Clemson to learn more about the Tigers, junior linebacker Eldridge Milton filled their notebooks.

"We don't want to just win; we want to kill people…We want to blow people out by forty or fifty points…We want to shut people out and run the score up on them as much as we can. We want to be recognized, and to do that we want to embarrass people."

The root of these bold words was a conversation Ford had with his players a few days earlier, telling them the only way for Clemson to earn a national title without appearing in a bowl was to impress voters with lopsided victory margins during the regular season.

The lofty rankings made Ford a bit uncomfortable because in previous years the Tigers rallied around the belief that everyone on the outside was underestimating them. Now, everyone on the outside was deeming them fit for greatness.

After a 40-7 win over Appalachian State in the opener, Clemson went to Virginia to face a team that entered the season with abundant optimism under third-year coach George Welsh.

The Tigers took great joy in pounding the Cavaliers 55-0, and Ford left his starters in far longer than he had to as Clemson claimed its twentieth consecutive ACC victory. Virginia finished the season with eight wins and a Top Twenty ranking.

Clemson rolled up 535 yards of offense and tacked on a touchdown with forty-four seconds left. No one considered apologizing for it after the game. Virginia was viewed as one of the ringleaders in the extra punishment from the ACC, and now the Tigers were returning the favor with some extra punishment on the football field.

"We're mad," junior defensive back Kenny Danforth told reporters. "We're on probation, and feel we got a rough deal. So when we play, we're going to let people know we think we got a raw deal. We're mad, so why not be mad at everyone?"

Clemson took a number two ranking into its next game at number twenty Georgia. The Tiger Band held up a sign at Sanford Stadium that read "On Probation and Still Kickin," and by halftime the Tigers had done plenty of kicking, with a 20-6 lead.

But in a sloppy game that featured twelve combined turnovers (eight interceptions, four fumbles), the Bulldogs battled back and broke a 23-23 tie when Kevin Butler grooved a sixty-yard field goal.

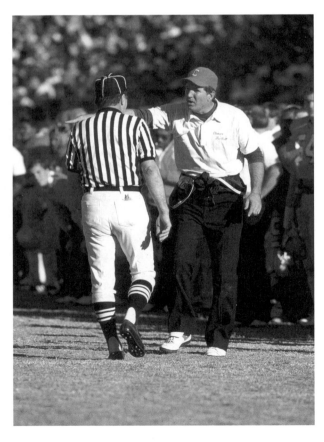

Ford questions a referee during a home game in the mid-1980s. *Courtesy of Clemson University Sports Information Department.*

Georgia play-by-play man Larry Munson said the stadium was "worse than bonkers" after Butler's kick. "This is ungodly," he told his listeners.

Ford on Butler's kick: "I guess that youngster busted that ball when he kicked it sixty yards. It's probably flat now."

Eleven seconds remained, and Clemson had an opportunity for a miracle on the kickoff when Terrance Roulhac took a cross-field pass from Ray Williams and found loads of running room behind a cluster of blockers. Roulhac was forced out of bounds at the Georgia thirty-five, and time expired. Clemson's sideline believed there was one second left when Roulhac stepped out. A flag was thrown on the Clemson sideline after the play was blown dead.

Ford protested and demanded an explanation, but none was given.

"I thought there was one second on the clock when our boy went out of bounds on the kickoff, and there was also a flag thrown for a late hit," Ford told reporters after the game. "I tried to find the official but couldn't. Don't get me wrong: Don't print that I said the officials messed up, because I don't know if they did or not. I just wanted to know."

A day later, the Tiger Band was in Atlanta to perform at the Houston-Atlanta NFL football game. When the band broke into "Tiger Rag," the crowd at Fulton County Stadium gave a rude reception by hurling jeers and taunts.

Clemson's entourage was back in Atlanta the next week for the Tigers' first visit to Georgia Tech with the Yellow Jackets members of the ACC. Longtime Tigers fans called Grant Field "Grant's Tomb," referring to a load of losses there when the Yellow Jackets were a national power and Clemson was considered too puny to merit regular visits from the Yellow Jackets.

Clemson carried a twenty-game ACC winning streak into the game, one short of the conference record held by Maryland. The streak died as the number eighteen Jackets beat the number thirteen Tigers 28-21. Georgia Tech coach Bill Curry, whose team had already beaten Alabama, called this the biggest win of his career at the time.

Clemson fell behind 21-0 and battled back to tie it at 21 before allowing the Jackets to drive fifty-four yards for the game-winning touchdown. Fullback Chuck Easley scored from a yard out with thirty-three seconds left.

The seniors voted to wear orange pants for the next game, a visit from North Carolina, but Ford vetoed it. Clemson won 20-12, defeating the Tar Heels for a fourth straight season, as senior defensive tackle William Perry dominated the fourth quarter. The Tigers struck for a huge fourth-quarter touchdown on a seventy-six-yard strike from Mike Eppley to Roulhac.

Ford complained about the officiating after the game, saying the refs needed to "get to hustling."

"Our supervisor needs to take some kind of action, and that's not just this football game. It's all football games when they don't hustle and do their job. And I don't care if they don't like me no more anyway. I've been trying to be just as good as I could be with them. It's just amazing some of the things that's going on out there that's not getting called and then some of the things that's getting called that's not happening."

On the same day of Clemson's win over the Tar Heels, Georgia beat Alabama 24-14 in Birmingham to heighten the pressure on Crimson Tide coach Ray Perkins. An airplane flew over Legion Field dragging a banner that called for Alabama to hire Ford, an Alabama alumnus. Ford dismissed the speculation that he'd leave for the Crimson Tide, where he played for Bear Bryant in the 1960s.

In the next game against Duke, Clemson answered critics who said the offense was too stale and conservative. The Tigers won 54-21, scoring on their first nine possessions with an array of halfback passes, deep throws and other unconventional tactics. Perry became the school's all-time leader in career sacks and tackles for loss.

Ford earned his fiftieth career coaching victory in the next game, a 35-34 win at N.C. State, but he didn't consider it particularly special given the difficulty Clemson had defeating the Wolfpack. N.C. State ripped apart the Tigers' defense over the first three quarters, taking advantage of poor tackling. Midway through the second quarter, a Wolfpack linebacker intercepted a pass and took it eighty-one yards for a touchdown that put Clemson in a 24-14 hole.

Eppley helped the Tigers rally by capitalizing on two turnovers early in the third quarter, and with the late lead Ford made a decision to punt after a drive stalled at State's thirty-four with 1:39 on the clock. Dale Hatcher made a perfect punt, pinning the Wolfpack at its own four.

Ford said the decision "made us look a whole lot smarter," but he was still trying to figure out how his team let the Wolfpack recover from a 35-24 deficit.

"I can remember when Clemson had a lead of 10 points, you could sit down and feel good," he told reporters at Carter-Finley Stadium. "Not today."

The uneasiness at Clemson was compounded by what was unfolding in Columbia. South Carolina was putting together a dream season under second-year coach Joe Morrison, having started 7-0 with major victories over Georgia, Pittsburgh and Notre Dame. Two days after his team's narrow win in Raleigh, Ford made an appearance at the Greenville Touchdown Club and said the Tigers were "third-page news," a mere footnote compared to the Gamecocks' success story.

The unranked Tigers returned home and coasted to a 37-14 win over Wake Forest after scoring 27 first-half points, improving to 6-2.

Ford's team found itself in a difficult struggle the next week against visiting Virginia Tech but managed to pull out a 17-10 win despite being outgained in all offensive statistics. Clemson had just eight first downs and trailed 10-7 for much of the game, but the Hokies missed two field goals and tossed an interception inside the Tigers' ten-yard line.

Foster Senn, a columnist for the *Tiger*, chastised the team's inconsistency in effort and attitude in a column the next week.

> *What is disappointing and disturbing is the unspoken attitude of the players. For two years now the team has played only when it wants. Last year the games Clemson really came to play in can be counted on six fingers. This year it's turned out to be the same story...For the past two years the same old line has been heard time and time again—no bowl, no motivation. Whatever happened to college spirit and playing for the pride of your school? Whatever happened to going out and playing your best the whole game, not just in the fourth quarter?*

A week later, Clemson traveled to Baltimore and ran into a Maryland team that was just as hungry as the Tigers were a year earlier in a 52-27 annihilation of the Terrapins. According to an article in a Baltimore newspaper, the two teams crossed paths at the Raleigh-Durham airport in late October after Clemson's win over N.C. State and Maryland's victory at Duke. The article said the Tigers taunted the Terrapins by pointing to their championship rings and reminding them of the blowout in 1983.

Maryland was plenty motivated and full of confidence after an unthinkable comeback against Miami a week earlier. Quarterback Frank Reich engineered a 42-40 victory in the Orange Bowl, somehow pulling the Terps out of a 31-0 hole against the Hurricanes.

Clemson lost 41-23, and it was the manner by which the Tigers lost that bothered Ford the most. Maryland bludgeoned his team up front on both sides of the ball, rushing for 406 yards and totaling thirty-five first downs.

Ford on the sidelines during a game at Georgia Tech, possibly during the 1984 season when the Yellow Jackets snapped the Tigers' twenty-game ACC winning streak. *Courtesy of Clemson University Sports Information Department.*

Getting beaten was bad enough to Ford. Getting physically manhandled was akin to torture. A reporter asked him about the gaping holes in the Tigers' defense.

"I don't know how to spell gaping," he replied, "but they were a mile wide."

Ford said it was the worst defense Clemson had played since 1980. A reporter told him defensive back Kenny Danforth said Maryland "wanted it more," and Ford fumed.

"You don't get whipped like we got whipped—that's got nothing to do with motivation. That goes back to pride and lining up and whipping somebody's fanny. Whether you're motivated or not, you get knocked around a bunch, you're going to come back and respond. Get tired of it and fight. I don't know that we ever fought in the second half."

On the same day Clemson was getting drilled in Baltimore, rival South Carolina was in nearby Annapolis suffering a colossal meltdown in a 38-21 loss at Navy. The defeat cost the number two Gamecocks a spot in the Orange Bowl, where Clemson had won a national title just three years earlier. The shocking development gave Clemson fans hope that they could close the 1984 season on a good note by taking out the shattered Gamecocks, who had to visit Death Valley.

Four days before the game, Ford put his players and coaches off-limits to the media for the rest of the week. Before the Gamecocks lost at Navy, Ford said, he planned to cancel his Tuesday press conference and let South Carolina attract all the rivalry-week publicity.

"They were going to come in here and we were going to ambush them," he said. "After we lost, I figured I had to show up."

Another reason for the gag order was Ford's disappointment with some of his players' quotes before and after the Maryland defeat. He was tired of seeing his players make excuses in the media, and he also believed the press was distorting their quotes.

Ford tried to inspire the fans to create an imposing environment for the Gamecocks, who were still dealing with the devastation of the Navy defeat. There was still plenty for Clemson to play for; the Tigers were unbeaten in their previous twenty-six home games, and they'd beaten the Gamecocks in four straight seasons.

"They will be coming over here trying to end a Clemson streak of wins over South Carolina, and right now I would say they have an excellent chance of doing it," Ford said. "If our people don't stand up and be counted, then they will win the football game—at Clemson…If we can't get ready to play this one, then we never had it in us to begin with."

The eighteen-point margin of defeat against Maryland was Clemson's worst in four years, and even as the rivalry game approached, the media wondered whether probation had sapped the motivation of the 1984 team.

Wrote Charles Bennett in the Anderson *Independent-Mail*: "Clemson coach Danny Ford said before the season started that the Tigers would be playing only for pride. There was a time when pride was enough."

The night before the game, thousands of copies of a fake "special edition" of the campus newspaper were distributed across Clemson featuring a blaring headline: "FORD TO BAMA?" Clemson officials had no idea where the papers came from. It was assumed that South Carolina fans were behind the prank.

Clemson conducted its pregame warm-ups in secrecy at the Jervey Athletic Facility and, minutes before kickoff, appeared at the top of the Hill wearing the sacred orange pants. The crowd was whipped into a frenzy, bringing back memories of the 1980 game against the Gamecocks when the Tigers wore orange pants for the first time.

Clemson roared to a 21-3 lead in the first half, and it seemed the Tigers' dominance over the Gamecocks would continue. But South Carolina's "Black Magic" returned as the Gamecocks rallied. Quarterback Mike Hold engineered a late touchdown drive, and a season that began with national title hopes ended with a soul-crushing 22-21 defeat and a final record of 7-4. After losing a total of two games over the previous three seasons, the Tigers doubled that number in 1984 and fell far short of the national title expectations that were rampant during the summer.

Ford walked into an interview room after the game and propped his bare feet onto a table. The sounds from the Gamecocks' wild celebration pulsed through the walls underneath the west end zone stands. Ford spent much of the season criticizing his team's spirit and motivation, but he couldn't bring himself to do it at this moment.

We're very proud of our seniors for what they have accomplished and for the kind of job they've done at Clemson. I told them that because I really mean it. Today, I feel very, very sorry for them...Our football team played very, very well. I don't doubt their courage. I don't doubt their 'want-to.' I don't doubt their being in the football game. I think they were mentally in the football game, emotionally in the football game. I just think we came up a little short.

The first loss in the orange pants, the first home defeat since 1980 and the first loss to the Gamecocks since 1979 made it feel like the sad passing of an era. But the end of probation was near as well, and that brought some relief and hope amid the tears and silence of the Tigers' locker room.

Ford did not want to talk about probation so soon after the defeat, allowing only that the Tigers would "start trying to become a better football team Monday."

"Right now, probation is not a very important word to me right now," Ford told reporters. "The loss to South Carolina is something I hate to see our players go through."

In an Associated Press article that appeared the next day, longtime sports information director Bob Bradley reflected on the passing of probation's dark cloud and the stigma that accompanied it.

"We're scot-free after January 2nd. It will keep everybody from sniping at us. There's always some people who take delight out of sniping at us. You look at the ACC standings and it shows Clemson with zero-zero-zero with a note that we're on probation."

Chapter 8
1985

Danny Ford and Clemson didn't experience a particularly lengthy period of relief after the conclusion of a three-year probation.

As the calendar turned to 1985, the university community was reeling from December revelations that SLED was investigating the athletics department for the illegal dispensing of prescription medications.

The investigation followed the passing of all-American cross-country athlete Augustinius Jaspers, who was found dead in his dorm room in late October 1984. Initially, the death was attributed to a heart defect, but chemists at SLED found traces of painkillers in Jaspers's blood.

Two track coaches, Stanley Narewski and Sam Colson, were suspended in December after university president Bill Atchley asked SLED to investigate "allegations of possible wrongdoing by two university employees." The two coaches later resigned and issued statements admitting they provided drugs to Clemson track athletes.

"The investigation involves the alleged dispensing of prescription medications to some student athletes in the track program, an idea which Clemson University will not permit to exist even at the level of gossip and innuendo," Atchley said in a news release.

Ford and his program were drawn into the controversy on January 20, when a former student assistant strength coach named Jack Harkness told the *Greenville News* that he distributed steroids to five Clemson football players.

Harkness had left Clemson in mid-December and returned to his home in Ontario to avoid prosecution. Harkness told the *Greenville News* that Colson instructed him to make the drug available to football players. He said he gave small quantities of steroids to four Clemson football players in the spring and fall of 1984.

"I think that was the whole key to it," Harkness told the newspaper. "It was there if they wanted it."

The *Greenville News* quoted an unidentified football player saying between five and fifteen players on the football team, mostly offensive linemen, used steroids that were acquired "somewhere in Jervey." SLED expanded its investigation to include all athletes at Clemson.

Ford and others in the football program were enraged and vehemently disputed the newspaper's characterization of Harkness as a football coach who worked closely with the program. Ford issued a statement in response to the article, which was topped with a headline: "Football players got steroids from coaches."

> *The Greenville News story implies significant involvement of our football coaches with the distribution of steroids. That is totally false. Everyone I talked to read the headlines to mean football coaches were giving players steroids. The Greenville News throughout this story implies that football coaches are involved and this is a lie. Our program does not believe in, give advice about, or even suggest the use of steroids to our players. I assure the parents of our current players and the parents of the players we are recruiting that we have never suggested to our players that they use any drug to become bigger or better football players. Winning is certainly not that important.*

Ford went on to say Harkness was "never a football coach of any kind" and was nothing more than a graduate assistant in the weight room.

The overall prescription-drug scandal exacerbated the power struggle between Atchley and longtime athletics director Bill McLellan. When McLellan first heard rumblings about his track coaches dispensing painkillers, he planned an internal investigation. He was angered when Atchley stepped in and called on SLED to take over.

McLellan, who had faced considerable scrutiny from the school's faculty in the aftermath of football probation, was the target of more criticism. He was blasted for letting the athletics department tarnish the reputation of the university as a whole, and in February, the faculty senate voted 19-5 to express lack of confidence in McLellan. A second faculty organization followed suit, expressing no confidence in the athletics director and saying he "has done irreparable harm to Clemson University."

McLellan's growing number of critics argued that he was the common denominator in the three scandals that had engulfed the athletics department over the previous decade—major recruiting violations in the basketball program in the mid-1970s, major recruiting violations in football in the late 1970s and early 1980s and now this.

The IPTAY board remained staunchly supportive of McLellan, as did some influential members of the board of trustees. Charles Bennett of the Anderson *Independent-Mail* wrote in February that McLellan was "in the opinion of many, the most effective athletic director Clemson has ever had, and the growth of Clemson sports would seem to support the assumption."

In mid-February, McLellan requested a leave of absence pending the drug investigation. Associate athletics director Bobby Robinson was named acting head. Dean Cox, head of student affairs, told reporters that McLellan was not in danger of losing his job.

McLellan was a Clemson man who had played football for Frank Howard and was groomed by Howard to run the athletics department. When Charley Pell abruptly left for Florida in December 1978, McLellan quickly named Ford the successor and remained close with the Tigers' football coach.

In late February, the *State* newspaper ran an article on its front page quoting unnamed members of the board of trustees who said Atchley was losing support with "middle-ground trustees" who had backed him in the past. Of the thirteen-member board, seven votes were required to dismiss Atchley. The article said the necessary votes were there.

Clemson's faculty senate condemned any movement to fire Atchley. David Senn, president of the group, said it would be "sending a message that athletics is at least as important—or more important—than academics." The senate voted 30-3 to support Atchley. The *Greenville*

News also sided with Atchley and criticized the trustees in an editorial for favoring "the nurture, promotion and protection of athletics over the school's chartered purposes of teaching, research and public service."

The tug-of-war at Clemson was occurring when college presidents across the country were attempting to restore academic integrity and take the power away from alumni and trustees who cultivated an alleged win-at-all-costs culture. In late February, NCAA executive director Walter Byers said the College Presidents' Commission on Intercollegiate Athletics was poised to bring college athletics "back to the original intent." He also gave support to a plan that would "ostracize" colleges with "chronic" series of violations.

Southern Methodist University's football program was seven months from being hammered with a three-year probation after the discovery of recruiting violations involving an assistant coach and several boosters. Former Mustang lineman Sean Stopperich claimed that SMU paid him large sums of money to back out of an oral commitment to Pittsburgh, his hometown school. The Mustangs were banned from bowl games in 1985 and 1986 and banned from live television in 1986.

On Friday, March 1, the board of trustees met in Columbia and spent seven hours in executive session. Atchley demanded a vote of confidence during this meeting and informed the board that he planned to reassign McLellan to a non-athletics post at the university. Atchley, who had served as president since 1979, told the board he feared Clemson would become known as "Clemson Athletic University" and said public opinion was "hanging like a sword over the head of" the school. The board denied Atchley's request, and he resigned. Cox later became interim president.

Dan Foster of the *Greenville News* wrote that certain trustees never forgave Atchley for trying to run the athletics department and were determined to "get him some time, some way, somewhere."

"The biggest mistake Bill Atchley made was thinking when the Clemson board of trustees told him they wanted him to be the school president, that they meant it," Foster wrote.

Atchley's ouster was a testament to the immense power McLellan had built at Clemson, but he wouldn't last much longer either. In late July, the *State* reported that the board of trustees approved the forced retirement of McLellan "for the good of Clemson." A source told the newspaper that

McLellan's departure was necessary "to settle things down on campus, because no matter where he is placed, his presence is going to be felt because of his past authority and influence."

When McLellan took over as athletics director in 1971, Clemson's football stadium seated forty-three thousand. Three expansions pushed capacity to eighty-two thousand by the 1983 season. Varsity sports increased from eight to seventeen under his leadership. IPTAY brought in $400,000 in 1971 and more than $5 million in 1984.

When he met with the ACC media in late July at Pinehurst Resort in North Carolina, Ford was in good spirits. "We're free," the coach said, referring to the end of probation. "We're going to try to play football and try to compete."

The Tigers lost a large number of players from the 1984 team that finished 7-4, and the inexperience made Ford antsy about 1985. Maryland was picked to win the ACC.

In mid-August, Ford announced he was restricting media access to his team. The Tigers' locker room would no longer be open to the press after games, and the only players available for interviews would be those he personally selected. Ford told reporters he believed they "take advantage" of his players. He also said he didn't want some players speaking with the media after games because "a lot of times the players don't know what they're talking about." The measures were considered extreme in an era of open media access to college programs.

Bobby Robinson, preparing for his first season as athletics director, told the *Greenville News:* "I told him we don't have a policy. He shouldn't have said that. I'll have the final say on the matter. But if Danny's plan is sound, I'll go along with it." Ford was informed of Robinson's quote and responded: "I told him what we're going to do and that's the way we're going to do it."

Clemson had some strong pieces returning. The running back position was loaded with Kenny Flowers, Stacey Driver and Terrence Flagler. Michael Dean Perry, younger brother of William "the Refrigerator" Perry, was entering his sophomore season.

The feeling among players was that Clemson football was back, poised to dominate the ACC and contend for major bowls again. But the Tigers had major holes on the offensive line, and the two-deep chart released the week of their opener at Virginia Tech featured sixteen sophomores and redshirt freshmen. Clemson was not ranked in the preseason Top Twenty of either the AP or UPI polls.

Sophomore quarterback Randy Anderson entered August camp as the starting quarterback, but redshirt freshman Rodney Williams was contending for the job vacated by Mike Eppley. Four days before the opener, Ford told the media he didn't know what to think about this team and said it was a "peculiar" season.

The opener at Virginia Tech was played under odd circumstances. Almost a fourth of the 31,110 fans were Clemson supporters. Because school wasn't yet in session in Blacksburg, the Tiger Band played the national anthem before the game and performed the halftime show.

The trip ended happily courtesy of a scrawny, anonymous kicker from Jacksonville named David Treadwell, who kicked a thirty-six-yard field goal after time expired to give the Tigers a 20-17 victory.

A forty-one-yarder by Treadwell had fallen short as the clock struck zero, but he was given a reprieve when Morgan Roane was penalized for roughing the kicker. The second try barely cleared the crossbar.

Treadwell didn't even have a bio in the 1985 media guide. The only mention of him was a small mug shot under the heading "Veteran Tiger Reserves." Ford said after the game he wasn't even sure how Treadwell ended up with the football program.

A redshirt sophomore who walked on to the football team, Treadwell was a soccer standout in high school but hadn't played organized football since grammar school. He spent the previous two years learning from Bob Paulling, Dale Hatcher and Donald Igwebuike at practice.

Ford spent time working with Treadwell before the 1985 season, making him kick from different parts of the field and presenting various distractions. Treadwell didn't know the kicking job was his until the second quarter of this game, when Ford told him he needed to prepare to kick the extra point as the offense advanced deep into Hokies territory.

Asked after the game what he told Treadwell before the game-winning kick, Ford said: "I just told him to go kick the football, we'd go get on the plane and go home and have champagne."

Ford was nevertheless frustrated after watching his team total six fumbles, five of which were lost. Up 17-10 with 6:09 left, Flagler fumbled away the ball on the Clemson seventeen-yard line. Virginia Tech then tied the score on a fourth-and-fifteen touchdown pass from Clemson's twenty-two.

Next was a visit from Georgia, and the typical heavyweight buildup was diminished for this meeting because both teams had dipped to seven wins the previous year. The Tigers and Bulldogs were both inexperienced and rebuilding in 1985.

Before the game, Clemson cheerleaders carried a large orange casket to midfield. The word "Probation" was printed on the side. The Tiger mascot burst out, shattering the box as a cannon fired simultaneously.

Clemson was up 10-3 entering the fourth quarter, but Georgia scored seventeen fourth-quarter points to win at Death Valley for the first time since 1976. Two years earlier, the Bulldogs forged a similar late rally for a 16-16 tie on the Tigers' home field.

The Tigers didn't seem all that devastated in the locker room after the 20-13 defeat. Clemson had gone four consecutive seasons without a win over the Bulldogs, who rushed for 360 yards on this day.

Georgia Tech visited Death Valley the next week and handed Clemson a 14-3 loss. The Tigers had suffered three straight home defeats for the first time since 1975 and seemed a long, long way from their dominating ways.

Clemson crossed midfield just twice in the second half, and the final score would've been more decisive if not for three missed field goals by the Yellow Jackets. The Tigers' fourteen-game home winning streak against ACC competition was snapped, and Ford began to second-guess his decision to throw the ball more in 1985.

For the first time since 1979, the Tigers didn't score a touchdown. The only points were a second-quarter field goal of 25 yards by Treadwell. Clemson entered the Georgia Tech game averaging 141 yards rushing, a figure that disgusted Ford. The Tigers finished with 101 against the Yellow Jackets.

"This is undoubtedly the sorriest-coached football game I've ever coached," Ford told reporters after the game. "I think that pretty much explains our performance. It was a total failure as a football team offensively. I don't think that's hard to say. But I don't want to fuss on our people. They just don't know how to play football very well at this point."

Ford was asked how much of the loss could be pinned on Anderson, who was struggling as quarterback.

"Don't start asking that (expletive)," he snapped. "You've got to *block*. We didn't do it. You've got to control the football like we haven't done, then you've got to *protect*. And then you've got to stand in the pocket and throw. I will do the blaming."

Things got worse in a 26-7 defeat at Kentucky that saddled Ford with his first three-game losing streak as the Tigers' coach. Kentucky's prolific quarterback, Bill Rasdell, missed the game after suffering a punctured lung on the first play from scrimmage. The Wildcats still had no problem moving the ball, going up 16-0.

The Tigers racked up seven turnovers, including three in the fourth quarter. Twice, Ford's team was penalized for interfering with fair catches on punts as it fell to 1-3.

The lead paragraph from Ron Green in the *Greenville News* the next day: "There's trouble in Tigertown. Big trouble."

The next week, Ford urged his team to loosen up as it prepared for a visit from Virginia. He said the Tigers had nothing to lose with a 1-3 record, and he wanted them to have some fun. They had amassed eighteen turnovers in four games.

Clemson held on for a 27-24 win, improving to 25-0 all-time over the Cavaliers. Rodney Williams started for the first time and guided the offense on three long drives as the Tigers pulled off what some people called an upset. Clemson committed just one turnover while running a steady array of sweeps, option and reverses.

As the Tigers were preparing for a game at Duke, Max Lennon was named president of the university. Lennon, who had served as an administrator at Ohio State, said he would "strive to continue to place emphasis on academics." He said Clemson's trustees assured him they would not meddle in his day-to-day affairs.

"I don't know that I've ever seen a more unified board," Lennon said at the time, "a board that's committed to developing policies that gives the freedom necessary to become excellent in the academic and athletic community. The only thing I require from them is unanimous support from the board."

Lennon also advocated "a commitment to bring the light of understanding rather than the heat of emotion to the discussion table."

The *Greenville News* ran an editorial that said Clemson was "entering a bright new era."

Duke was next. Blue Devils coach Steve Sloan had been quoted as saying he was looking forward to playing Clemson, and Ford said he didn't blame him.

"I'm not scared of Clemson," Ford said. "Kentucky wasn't. No one else has been, and I don't understand why they should be. And I'm sure he's seeing the same thing we're seeing. They look forward to playing Clemson and so do 110 other major universities."

Clemson won 21-9 after scoring three times in the first half and holding off the Blue Devils after halftime.

The Tigers played host to N.C. State the next week, and Wolfpack coach Tom Reed was under major fire with a 1-6 record. His chancellor, Bruce Poulton, told N.C. State's student senate the week of the game that he wouldn't care if the university dropped the football program.

Clemson won easily, 39-10, thanks in part to an overwhelming performance by Michael Dean Perry. The defense had five sacks in the first quarter and intercepted four passes for the game. The Tigers had rushed for 276 yards a game in their previous three games after averaging 131 in their first four.

The Tigers beat Wake Forest 26-10 the next week at Death Valley, outgaining the Demon Deacons 472-285. Clemson had won four consecutive games after its 1-3 start, and a major reduction in turnovers helped fuel the turnaround.

With two ACC games remaining—at North Carolina and Maryland at home—Clemson could do no worse than a tie for the conference crown if it beat the Tar Heels and Terrapins.

The Tigers had won a combined nineteen straight games over North Carolina's "Big Four" schools, and Ford was 5-1 against the Tar Heels. Clemson also hadn't lost at Kenan Stadium since 1971.

The streaks ended in controversy when North Carolina used a questionable call by officials to win 21-20. A twelve-yard pass from Jonathan Hall to Quinton Smith was ruled a completion late, giving the Tar Heels a first-and-goal from the one with less than two minutes left.

Smith leaped over Perry Williams to snare the ball, but he dropped it on the hit. North Carolina cashed in with a touchdown.

Tim Ellerbe, columnist for the *Independent-Mail,* wrote the next day: "From an end-zone vantage point, the pass was dropped. It was incomplete."

Immediately after the game, Ford was less than irate as he reflected on the call. He was more perturbed about the officials' inability to control a game that featured numerous late hits and other assorted nastiness between the two rivals. He was also upset that his defense allowed Hall, a freshman making his first college start, to move the Tar Heels on 80- and 70-yard scoring drives in the fourth quarter.

Down 7-0 at halftime, Clemson rallied to take a 17-7 lead before North Carolina took control in the fourth. To Dan Foster of the *Greenville News,* the biggest story of the day was the bitter hostility on display between the two teams.

> *Everyone within shouting distance of the series knows it. The slightest contact between players that was not absolutely essential to the play Saturday was an act of war. The press box counted seven identifiable post-play "confrontations." Only one met the standard for player ejections, one from each team. Others could have. If a vote were taken among the Tar Heels players as to bowl ambitions, it might be a dead heat whether they would rather go to one or keep Clemson out of one.*

Virginia lost to N.C. State on the same day, meaning the Tigers (5-4, 4-2 ACC) lost an opportunity to win the conference title outright by falling in Chapel Hill. The Tar Heels ended up finishing the season with a 5-6 record.

Maryland brought a strong team to Death Valley the next week. The Terps, whose only losses that season were to three teams (Penn State, Miami, Michigan) that finished in the Top Ten, were 5-0 in the ACC and attempting to win the conference title.

Clemson was an eight-point underdog, and Ford said going in there was no question Maryland was the best team in the conference.

Down 24-14 at one point thanks in part to two early blocked punts by the Tigers, Maryland erupted for 17 fourth-quarter points to win. And after Dan Plocki kicked a twenty-yard field goal with three seconds left to put the Terps up 34-31, Ford lost it.

Ford argues with referees near the end of Clemson's narrow loss to Maryland late in the 1985 season. *Courtesy of Clemson University Sports Information Department.*

Minutes earlier, Maryland committed what Ford and Clemson fans believed to be three infractions on the game-tying touchdown pass from Stan Gelbaugh to Ferrell Edmunds: an offensive lineman appeared to move before the snap, Edmunds dropped the ball an instant after he corralled Gelbaugh's pass in the end zone and the twenty-five-second play clock appeared to run out before the ball was snapped.

No call was made, and the two-yard touchdown pass stood. Ford stormed onto the field after Plocki's field goal, venturing all the way to the five-yard line where the officials were huddled. A CBS microphone picked up Ford's tirade. He was going after Dan Post, the official who made the controversial call against the Tigers a week earlier in Chapel Hill.

Ford: "We've been screwed! You missed a call last week on the sideline. The twenty-five-second went off here. I saw the son of a (expletive)!"

Clemson was penalized fifteen yards for unsportsmanlike conduct before the kickoff, and a tense situation deteriorated into a melee when Maryland defensive back Lewis Askew forced Terrance Roulhac out of bounds on the Clemson sideline to end the game. Askew was surrounded by at least five Clemson players, and replays showed him being struck by punches. Defensive lineman Raymond Chavous, linebacker Terence Mack and grad assistant David Bennett came to Askew's defense and helped diffuse the situation as fans swarmed onto the field.

Ford barred the media from speaking with his players after losing a game that could have made the Tigers' season. He apologized for the fight, calling Maryland a "class program," but he unloaded on the officiating. His biggest problem was the referees' inability to see the expiration of the play clock.

Ford had harsh words on his postgame radio show.

One of them is not a judgment call and our supervisor of officials is going to have a hard time explaining to me how I can get fired for not

Ford is enraged that referees failed to spot the expiration of the play clock moments before Maryland scored a late touchdown.
Courtesy of Clemson University Sports Information Department.

winning football games…and the official can blow a call and call again
the next week, and call again the next year…He tells me this is his best
crew down here to work the two hardest games we've got a chance to play.
And if that's their best crew then we need some substitutes in the officials.

The late-game controversy and fisticuffs were big news the next day. CBS replayed the embarrassing ending on its NFL pregame show. Ford drove to Charlotte for a Sunday meeting with the ACC's supervisor of officials and said the conversation "made my day."

Next for the Tigers was a trip to Columbia to face rival South Carolina, and an Independence Bowl bid was at stake for two 5-5 teams. But on the Clemson end, the entire week was filled with fallout from Maryland.

In the Tuesday papers, Clemson officials said they were "deeply embarrassed" by the conduct of Ford and members of the football team. Nick Lomax, acting vice president for student affairs, announced he was conducting an investigation and predicted "some action to come out of this."

"We are embarrassed by (Ford) going on the field," Lomax told reporters. "We are embarrassed by the fight."

At his Tuesday press conference, Ford vowed to discipline players who threw punches and commended the three members of his team who protected Askew.

Regarding the profanity that was captured by CBS microphones: "I wish I did not say an ugly word. I'm not proud of saying that. I don't want to be embarrassing to my family but I can't wear a piece of tape on my mouth to coach."

Tim Ellerbe of the *Independent-Mail* wrote that Ford blew up "at a God-awful time…Clemson, after suffering through probations and a prescription drug controversy, has tried extremely hard in the past eight months to build a new image. This did not help."

As Ford was taking part in his press luncheon, high-level Clemson administrators were meeting with ACC officials in Charlotte and watching the fight from various camera angles provided by footage from CBS. Ford was informed later that day that penalties would be announced late Wednesday afternoon.

In a joint action between the ACC and Clemson, Ford and six players were disciplined. Ford was given an official reprimand, a one-year "probation," and was barred from the sideline of the Tigers' 1986 game at Maryland.

Defensive players Norman Haynes, Eric Dawson, Kenny Danforth and James Lott were suspended for the South Carolina game. Danforth had started seven games at strong safety and totaled fifty-three tackles. Haynes and Dawson had played in all ten games. Lott was being redshirted as a freshman and had not played.

Ford issued a statement apologizing for the incidents. He later declined comment as he tried to turn the focus to the Gamecocks, who'd beaten his team by a point the previous year in Death Valley. The Tigers were also dealing with a number of injuries, including one that would keep star defensive lineman Michael Dean Perry out of the rivalry game.

Both the Gamecocks and Tigers were trying to close disappointing seasons on a positive note. South Carolina slid dramatically after a ten-win season in 1984, suffering blowout defeats to Michigan, Georgia, Pittsburgh and Florida State while losing at home to a bad N.C. State team and struggling to outlast Appalachian State and Navy.

High above Williams-Brice Stadium on game day, an airplane dragged a banner with the message, "Talk Dirty To Me Danny: Go Terps."

Clemson fell behind 14-3 early but rebounded to tie the score at halftime. The Tigers gained more of the momentum after recovering a fumble by Kent Hagood on the first play of the second half.

A late field goal by Treadwell put Clemson up 24-17, and Perry Williams made an interception of Mike Hold deep in Tigers territory to preserve the win.

"We needed to win this game because they beat us last year," Ford said after the game. "We don't need to lose two in a row to South Carolina in the state, for recruiting and all that sort of thing. This was the biggest ballgame we've had in quite a while."

Ford was more than happy to accept a bid to play Minnesota in the Independence Bowl. A 6-5 record fell far short of the standard that had been set at Clemson, and Shreveport wasn't exactly considered an ideal postseason destination.

Some people suggested Ford decline the invitation and keep Clemson home for the holidays. But the Tigers hadn't been to a bowl since 1981, and Ford wanted to have some fun after three Christmases spent at home.

The 1985 team was full of young players who prepared for the bowl hoping to set a foundation for a return to prominence in future years. But on a cold December 21 night before 42,800 fans, a cold start by the Tigers ended up sealing their demise in a 20-13 defeat.

The Gophers were overseen by interim coach John Gutekunst, who stepped in when Lou Holtz took the job at Notre Dame. Gutekunst became the second coach in NCAA history to win a bowl game in his coaching debut. The first was Ford, who accomplished the feat in a 1978 Gator Bowl victory over Ohio State.

Clemson fell behind the Gophers 10-0 after committing three turnovers in the first seven minutes. The Tigers rallied to take a 13-10 lead in the third quarter on a pass from Stacey Driver to Keith Jennings, but Minnesota tied it on a field goal and then drove 68 yards in 11 plays for the decisive points with 4:56 left.

Rodney Williams had a poor passing game and was replaced by Randy Anderson at one point. The Tigers' defense was sliced up on the option by quarterback Rickey Foggie, who was from Laurens. Ford said after the game that the Tigers looked "like an early-season Clemson team rather than a late-season Clemson team."

Probation had finally caught up to Ford's program in 1984 and 1985, when the Tigers lost 10 games after amassing a 30-2-2 record from 1981 to 1983.

But even in the immediate aftermath of a sour closing to a 6-6 season, Ford and Clemson supporters knew brighter days were ahead.

Ford after the game: "Let's leave this one in 1985."

Chapter 9
1986

As Clemson's program moved further away from probation in early 1986, it was evident that Danny Ford was assembling the talent and the momentum for a return to greatness.

The 1985 team was filled with freshmen and juniors. Clemson fans remembered that the 1980 team was composed similarly, and that team's mediocrity gave way to years-long dominance starting with the 1981 national title.

One of Ford's main objectives entering 1986 was to protect the football. Clemson committed thirty-two turnovers in 1985, when four of its losses came by a combined eighteen points. After a failed attempt to incorporate more passing in 1985, Ford was getting back to his roots of ball-control offense, solid defense and a dependable kicking game.

"Instead of running an option drill at a manager, we're going to run it at a player," he said in the *Tiger* before spring practice. "We need to create more live situations in practice to cut down on our turnovers…Our number one priority this spring is to improve our option offense. We have to get the ball on the corners and execute the triple-option offense."

The June death of former Maryland basketball star Len Bias rocked the country and introduced drug use to the growing list of ills afflicting big-time college sports. Bias, who'd been selected number two overall by the Boston Celtics in the NBA draft, died of a cocaine overdose. Two

Maryland basketball players were indicted on drug charges in the wake of his death. Also during this period, three football players at Virginia faced cocaine trafficking charges.

Momentum for major NCAA reform was building as a result of pay-for-play scandals in college football and basketball. Overzealous boosters were blamed for destroying the system, and college presidents were compelled to rein in their athletics programs. The NCAA adopted new rules to punish repeat offenders, and in the summer of 1986, revelations were coming forth at SMU that would lead to the "death penalty" for the probation-plagued football program.

In late July at the summer ACC football media gathering, the discussion and headlines centered on everything but X's and O's. Ford's program was in the crosshairs of scrutiny after news broke in June that sexual assault accusations had been lodged against star tailback Kenny Flowers, who was considered a Heisman Trophy candidate entering the season.

A thirty-seven-year-old woman, the mother of a former Clemson player, alleged that Flowers, teammate A.J. Johnson and two former Tigers raped her at an off-campus apartment. The woman dropped the charges eighteen hours after the alleged incident, but she reopened the case a month later after meeting with an Anderson attorney.

Clemson went through August practice with the case still unresolved as thirteenth-circuit solicitor Joe Watson and the Clemson police department conducted an investigation. The woman had told police she was approached by a man at a service station and forced to drive to the apartment. One of the accused, former player Craig Crawford, told police the woman wanted to buy cocaine and participated in consensual sex in return for the drug. The woman was reported to have been drinking at the time of the crime she alleged.

When a group of ACC reporters visited Clemson in late August to get a preview of the 1986 football team, Ford was asked about the investigation.

"I know what I'd do if they were convicted of a crime. I've got my rules. But I'm not going to convict them. I'm not going to judge them. I don't know the facts. I'll agree with what the United States courts say."

On September 2, eleven days before Clemson's season opener against Virginia Tech, a Pickens County grand jury cleared Flowers and the other three men after finding no cause to indict on rape, kidnap and robbery charges. Flowers, Johnson, Crawford and Alexander Holloman testified on their own behalf at a private hearing before the sixteen-member grand jury.

The *Greenville News* accused Clemson of providing "a safety net" for its athletes.

> *The university position seems to be that, while it won't defend any student shown to have committed a crime or anyone on its payroll proved to have acted unprofessionally, it also won't take substantial action against those who seriously violate campus norms. More is expected of a reputable university, perhaps especially when star football players are involved and questions are raised as to whether they will be coddled by the administration.*

Outside the courthouse in Pickens, Flowers told the media that a weight had been lifted from his shoulders.

"Up until now it's been real rough. After today I'm just glad justice prevailed. We had great lawyers working for us and we knew it would end this way."

Ford told WSPA-TV: "It was a no-win situation because it involved our whole family of football at Clemson. We're very sorry the whole thing happened and hopefully now we can get on with our football season."

From the last two games of 1984 through the 1985 season, Clemson had won six games and lost eight. But after disappearing from the polls through the entire 1985 season, Clemson was back on the radar. The *New York Times* ranked Clemson number twelve in its preseason Top Twenty.

In a 2011 interview with Tigerillustrated.com, Ford recalled the feeling in the program as the Tigers moved past the muck of probation.

> *We felt things had started to come back up. You build a house, you have a foundation and our foundation was starting to get stronger because we had our scholarship numbers back. We were even with everybody else. And if we were even with everybody else in numbers, we knew*

Ford in a meeting room with his assistants. Tommy West (right) later became Clemson's head coach after the 1993 firing of Ford replacement Ken Hatfield. *Courtesy of Clemson University Sports Information Department.*

we'd be tougher than they were, more physical than they were and we knew we'd beat them in the fourth quarter. So naturally we felt our plan was working.

New secondary coach "Brother" Bill Oliver, who spent fourteen years coaching defensive backs at Alabama and Auburn earlier in his career, said entering the season that the players he inherited at Clemson were as talented and faster than any of the groups he had in nine years with the Crimson Tide. Veteran cornerbacks Perry Williams and Delton Hall were starters in 1985, but they entered 1986 as backups to sophomore Donnell Woolford and redshirt freshman James Lott. Clemson had fifty-two lettermen and fourteen starters returning.

As the season approached, administrators were discussing the prospect of a $4 million athletics dormitory. The university's faculty senate recommended that athletes not be housed separately from the regular student body and said a new dormitory would further isolate athletes from the mainstream campus population.

The *Tiger* supported a new dorm in an editorial. "Clearly, maintaining a separate dormitory for football players or even building a new football player dorm is an investment worth paying for."

Before the season, Ford took out an advertisement in the student newspaper seeking a punter. He found one when Bill Spiers, the starting shortstop for the baseball team, responded to the ad and won the job over twenty other students who showed up.

Flowers suffered a leg injury in practice two weeks before the opener, and Terrence Flagler started in his place against Virginia Tech. The Tigers had won nine straight over the Hokies dating to 1954, but Virginia Tech was a hungry and determined team entering Death Valley after suffering narrow defeats to the Tigers in 1985 and 1984.

Before the game, as Clemson's players gathered at the top of the Hill, Virginia Tech players stood below and taunted them. The Hokies ended up winning 20-14, and the Tigers had lost four of five games dating to the ninth game of the 1985 season.

Junior quarterback Erik Chapman had thirteen completions for 242 yards, burning the Tigers' secondary on deep play-action passes, and Virginia Tech blocked a Spiers punt and recovered it for a touchdown. Flowers fought through his injury to rush for 87 yards on twenty-two carries, but he was stopped for 3 yards on fourth-and-seven from Clemson's forty-six with 3:39 left.

Ford pointed the finger at himself and his staff for burning a valuable timeout in the fourth quarter when twelve men were on the field. "Ridiculous," he said after the game. "That's poor coaching, poor organization."

He also criticized his players for complacency and an inability to recognize the Hokies as a formidable foe. Virginia Tech went on to finish 9-2-1 in Bill Dooley's final season.

"We told our people for two years now that they are going to come in and knock our heads off. We've been lucky enough to win the football games in the past two years. This year, they came in and did the same thing, and we sat around waiting for something good to happen for us."

Tommy Trammell, sports columnist for the *Tiger*, ripped the team the next week as the Tigers prepared for a trip to Georgia. The Bulldogs had finished 7-3-1 the previous year and were ranked number fourteen. Not many Clemson supporters were optimistic enough to ponder the thought of a win in Athens after what they'd seen in the opener.

> *What has happened to the days when opponents dreaded a trip to Death Valley? Now we find the likes of the Hokies welcoming the Tigers down the hill for a beating...Plain and simple, the Tigers weren't ready to play on Saturday. There were defensive backs struggling to call defenses and get into position, there were players forgetting to report for special teams, and the Tigers seemed content to shift into cruise control and count on a big play to pull off the win.*

In Athens, coach Vince Dooley spent most of his weekly press conference cautioning against reading anything into Clemson's loss to Virginia Tech. He said the defeat "is just going to add fuel to the fire that's already burning inside Clemson and has been burning perhaps for all of last year."

Clemson fans were fretting about the possibility of an 0-3 start. After the trip to Georgia, the Tigers had to venture to Atlanta to face a Georgia Tech team that had dealt them painful defeats the previous two seasons. And Clemson's last victory over the hated Bulldogs, the 13-3 triumph in 1981, felt like ancient history.

Ford didn't seem all that optimistic at his Tuesday press conference, still brooding over the defeat that occurred three days earlier. He had family visiting from Alabama during the opening weekend, but he said the defeat ruined their visit.

"I didn't feel much like spending time with them. They wanted to go get some gas and I wouldn't even go pump gas. I didn't want to be seen, nor talked to, nor be around anybody. That's probably the first time I ever told Daddy I wasn't going to get him any gas. That's a fact. I told him to wait until the next morning."

It was hard to see a major turning point right around the corner. That turning point would come between the hedges at Sanford Stadium in front of an ABC split-national telecast. The Tigers announced their return to prominence with a nerve-jangling 31-28 victory that was sealed when David Treadwell sent a forty-six-yard field goal over the crossbar as time expired.

Ford and Georgia coach
Vince Dooley shake hands
before a game in Athens,
likely in 1986. Clemson
won that game 31-28 on
a late field goal by David
Treadwell. *Courtesy of
Clemson University Sports
Information Department.*

Clemson piled up 428 yards, 279 on the ground. All of that production seemed wasted when Georgia took over at its own twenty with 2:06 left and the score tied at 28. Everyone in the stadium thought back two years, when the Bulldogs drove far enough for a 60-yard field goal by Kevin Butler that provided a heart-stopping 26-23 triumph. But Clemson's defense held on this day, forcing a three-and-out and setting up the offense at its thirty-six with 1:11 on the clock. Quarterback Rodney Williams piloted a methodical drive into field goal range, and the Tigers called their final timeout with four seconds left.

The lanky Treadwell, a former walk-on who'd emerged from total obscurity in 1985, had hooked a thirty-nine-yard attempt earlier in the fourth quarter. Ford almost went with Rusty Seyle, who was better at long kicks. He opted for Treadwell because he was a shade quicker at getting off his kicks and Ford didn't want to risk a block.

Senior receiver Ray Williams was in tears after the game as he told reporters of a closed-door meeting that seniors had with Ford a few days earlier. He said finger-pointing was rampant after the opener, and the players didn't think the coaching staff believed in them.

"If we hadn't called the team meeting with the seniors last week, I'm not sure things would have changed at all," Williams told reporters at Sanford Stadium. "But we give this win to Coach Ford because he changed the attitude of the entire program."

Williams continued: "We're back. It's just as simple as that. We're back because this is going to turn the whole program around."

The Tigers gained even more momentum and confidence the next week by plowing through Georgia Tech in Atlanta, 27-3. Clemson ran for 283 yards thanks to monstrous holes provided by a line that was growing into a dominant unit. The offensive line had something to prove in 1986 after spending the previous season regarded as the offense's weak link, and it was young. Aside from senior Eric Nix and junior John Phillips, the line was filled with sophomores.

Flowers didn't run the ball in this game because of an ankle injury. Fullbacks Chris Lancaster and Tracy Johnson helped Clemson hold the ball for forty-one minutes. The Tigers ran eighty-six plays to Georgia Tech's fifty-one.

After a 24-0 win over the Citadel the next week, the Tigers moved into the AP poll at number twenty. The running success continued in a 31-17 win at Virginia when Flagler rushed for 210 yards on thirty carries.

The Tigers then smashed Duke 35-3 at Death Valley. Michael Dean Perry and the defense racked up fifteen tackles for loss and limited the Blue Devils to just sixteen rushing yards, and Flowers broke the career rushing record that had stood for twenty-four years. The senior finally was at 100 percent after dealing with nagging injuries dating to the summer.

During the game, a score from elsewhere blared through the PA system: N.C. State had upset North Carolina 35-34, leaving Clemson as the only remaining undefeated team in ACC play. The Tigers were 5-1 overall and full of confidence. Perry told reporters after the game that Clemson was ready to play Miami in the Orange Bowl for the national title.

The next test was in Raleigh, and in N.C. State the Tigers faced a dramatically improved team under first-year coach Dick Sheridan, a South Carolina graduate who had built Furman into a Division I-AA power. State, 4-1-1 and ranked in the Top Twenty, hadn't defeated Clemson since 1980.

On a dark, rainy afternoon at Carter-Finley Stadium, the Tigers fell apart by losing 27-3 before the CBS cameras. State torched Clemson's defense for several big plays, and Rodney Williams had a miserable day passing while completing just five of his twenty attempts. The Wolfpack shut down Clemson's inside running game, allowing linebackers to drop back and patrol passing lanes. In the *Tiger*, Phillips called it "the most complete beating I've ever been associated with."

Next up was a visit to Wake Forest, and Ford spent the week responding to growing criticism of Williams. The redshirt sophomore from Irmo wasn't a gifted passer and didn't look particularly graceful running the offense. In Columbia, freshman quarterback Todd Ellis was breaking passing records seemingly by the week for the rival Gamecocks.

Williams responded in a 28-20 victory in Winston-Salem. Matched opposite prolific Deacons quarterback Mike Elkins, Williams completed thirteen of nineteen passes for 192 yards and two touchdowns on his twenty-first birthday. Flagler amassed 273 all-purpose yards, setting a Clemson record. He ran for 209 and had 64 receiving yards while accounting for all four of the Tigers' touchdowns. Deacons coach Al Groh to reporters after the game: "If Kenny Flowers is a candidate for the Heisman Trophy, then Flagler is a candidate for Mr. Universe."

Ford was happy with the victory but said his team "played stupid at times." Clemson fumbled seven times, and Donnell Woolford mistakenly fielded two punts inside the five-yard line.

On this same day, Maryland coach Bobby Ross incited controversy when he chased down a referee and grabbed him after the Terps' 32-30 loss to North Carolina. Referee Don Safrit had mistakenly called for a timeout after a two-point conversion attempt, and Ross was enraged that Safrit failed to notify him that the Tar Heels still had a timeout remaining. North Carolina used the timeout to set up the game-winning field goal.

The ACC punished Ross by banishing him from the sideline of his team's upcoming home game against Clemson. That meant Ross and

Ford would both occupy the press box for the November 15 game in Baltimore. Ford's suspension was a result of his blowup late in a home loss to Maryland in 1985.

Before the visit to Maryland, Clemson still had a November 8 home clash against North Carolina and a renewal of a rivalry that had become bitter and nasty. The Tar Heels came in 5-2 and 3-1 in the ACC and were slight underdogs. Four days before the game, Ford touched on the clash of styles and cultures.

"You just say North Carolina is playing Clemson," he told reporters. "It's the orange versus the blue. That's all you've got to say. For some teams, you've got to say a lot of things. You've got to talk about their mommas and their brothers. This one you've just got to steer people in the right direction."

The morning of the game, it was announced that three Clemson players had been suspended for disciplinary reasons. Backup linebacker Rodney Curtis had been arrested six days earlier in Athens and charged with criminal attempt to rape and obstruction. He was suspended from the team pending the investigation. Receiver Terrance Roulhac and receiver Keith Jennings were suspended for an unrelated matter. It was speculated that they missed a team meeting during the week.

A year after losing by a point in Chapel Hill in controversial fashion, Clemson broke out the orange pants and left no doubt with a 38-10 thrashing. The Tigers also earned a share of the ACC title by virtue of Virginia's upset of N.C. State on the same day.

Williams executed the option flawlessly and helped the Tigers pile up 326 rushing yards. The defense dismantled a Tar Heels offense that had totaled more than 500 yards the previous week against Maryland.

The dominant storyline the week of the Maryland game was the coach-less teams. Ford and Ross tried to downplay the situation. With game-day temperatures predicted in the teens, Ford joked that at least he'd stay warm in the press box. "It's kind of funny," he told reporters, "but then again it ain't." NBC's "Today" show took interest in the odd arrangement and invited Ford and Ross to appear on the program Friday morning. Both coaches declined.

The Terps were out of the conference race and had a 4-5 overall record. But they were a week removed from a 17-15 loss at number three

Penn State, a team that would go on to win the national title, and Ford was concerned Clemson would have a difficult time in Baltimore.

The Tigers brought home the school's first official ACC title since 1982, but they secured it with a 17-17 tie that left Ford admitting he felt "a little empty." Down three with seven minutes left, Clemson took over at its eight-yard line. Williams drove the offense down the field, keeping the possession alive with a fourth-down pass to tight end Jim Riggs. Flagler had a chance to score on a pitch inside the five-yard line but was thrown for a loss. The final touchdown opportunity slipped through the Tigers' grasp when Williams threw low for Roulhac in the end zone with five seconds left. Treadwell kicked a twenty-one-yard field goal with two seconds on the clock.

"We don't recommend to our team to go for ties," Ford said afterward. "Only if it helps our program. Winning the conference championship when you're not picked to win one, we had no decision but to go for the field goal."

Next for the Tigers was the regular-season finale against South Carolina, and the Gamecocks were potent and formidable despite the 3-6-1 record they carried into Death Valley. "Don't get tied up in all that underdog crap," Ford told reporters the week of the game. "They're talented."

Under fourth-year coach Joe Morrison, the Gamecocks had shifted to a quirky "Run and Shoot" offense to maximize a fleet of talented skill players. South Carolina had come close to a far better season, suffering last-minute losses to Georgia, Nebraska and N.C. State in addition to a tie against Virginia Tech.

The Gamecocks ranked third nationally in passing with 291 yards per game by Ellis, the talented freshman. The Tigers ranked fifth nationally in rushing with 277 yards per game on the ground.

Clemson learned early in the week that it would face Stanford in the Gator Bowl, and Ford was worried players and fans would be distracted for the rivalry game. He said he'd

rather win this week than go to 10 Gator Bowls or Orange Bowls or Super Bowls. All roads lead to Saturday. We need another North Carolina week. We need more orange shakers, more enthusiasm from the student body. We need the faculty to let them out of class early. A loss against a home-state team hurts more than a loss at a bowl game or a win unless you're playing for all the marbles. This is the biggest one we've been in in a quite. We've got all the goody things and they've got all the poor-me things going for them.

A capacity crowd of more than eighty-one thousand showed at Death Valley for a matchup featuring two young and ascending programs. An estimated ten thousand people purchased tickets to watch the game on closed-circuit television at Carolina Coliseum in Columbia.

A long return by Roulhac on the opening kickoff set Clemson up for a quick touchdown, and after the Tigers turned a botched snap into a two-point conversion on the extra point try they were up 8-0 and everything was going their way.

The Gamecocks rebounded and took a 21-18 lead into halftime, punctuated by a sixty-one-yard interception return for a touchdown by Brad Edwards on a botched field goal try by the Tigers. Clemson had to drive to tie it at twenty-one with 2:50 left in the game after Ford elected to go for a field goal on fourth-and-one from South Carolina's fourteen-yard line. The Gamecocks swiftly drove into Clemson territory and were in position for the win, but Scott Hagler hooked a forty-one-yard field goal attempt with twenty-five seconds left. Ford called on Seyle to attempt a sixty-two-yarder as time expired, but it was ten yards short. The 21-21 tie, first between the rivals since 1950, made for a surreal scene in Clemson.

"It was just sort of a froze-up stadium," Ford said after the game. "Everybody just sat there and looked around and didn't know whether to jump up and holler or start crying. That's sort of the way our dressing room is at this point."

Wrote Herman Helms in the *State:* "Thus, the bragging rights go on ice for one whole year. Half of the citizens in a small state infatuated with college football won't be filled with joy and happiness, and the other half won't have to live in shame and pain. Instead, both sides will spend the winter frustrated."

Williams had a poor day against his hometown team, completing just six of nineteen pass attempts while facing heavy pressure. "It's depressing," Williams told reporters. "It's not what you work for all these weeks." Perry said this tie was "a little more sickening than Maryland was."

Ford and his team officially accepted the Gator Bowl bid in the locker room, and bowl chairman Henry Beckwith told the Tigers: "You'll forget about this one."

Big news broke in December when twelve players were suspended from bowl games after traces of steroids were found in testing by the NCAA. Clemson was one of twenty bowl teams tested, and the Tigers were clean. Two of Stanford's starting offensive linemen tested positive and were suspended.

In conjunction with Mazda's sponsorship of the Gator Bowl, both head coaches were given a Mazda vehicle of their choice for one year. Ford chose a four-wheel-drive, long-bed pickup truck.

An estimated forty thousand Clemson fans made the trip to Jacksonville for the December 27 bowl, and the Tigers' chances of a win appeared good when news broke that starting Cardinal quarterback John Paye, who earned second-team Pac-10 honors in 1986, was unavailable after undergoing shoulder surgery.

Clemson mauled Stanford in the first half, outgaining the Cardinal 291-57 and taking a 27-0 advantage into halftime. The Tigers were up 24-0 before Stanford registered a first down. Previously in 1986, no other team had scored 27 points on the Cardinal in an entire game.

At halftime, Ford told his players they'd do one of two things in the second half: continue to play well and pour on the points, or set an NCAA record for largest lead squandered in a bowl game. They came perilously close to suffering the latter fate. Stanford battled back, scoring three touchdowns to make it 27-21.

The masses of orange-clad fans present on this cool, overcast afternoon covered their eyes when the Cardinal took over at their own twenty-eight with 1:43 remaining in the game. The defense stiffened, preserving the victory as Clemson closed the season with an 8-2-2 record. Williams was all smiles as he received the MVP trophy at midfield.

Ford didn't spend much time at the postgame ceremony. He stalked off the field with his head down, cursing under his breath. This game seemed to mirror a season that contained glimpses of greatness, but also a season in which the Tigers had to hold on for dear life at the end.

Despite the conflicted feelings created by two ties and a near disaster in the final three games, the presence of so many young players produced abundant optimism for the future. The Tigers were on their way back.

Chapter 10
1987

For several years, with his football program facing repercussions from probation, Danny Ford sent a subtle but strong message to Clemson's competition.

"I remember it like it was yesterday," Ford recalled during a 2011 interview with Tigerillustrated.com. "I said: 'You better get us now because we're young and we're not going to be here long.'"

The Tigers were loaded. A large number of starters were back, and Clemson was quickly returning to college football's elite class.

The program's first big victory of 1987 came in February, when a decorated defensive end/linebacker recruit from Georgia named John Johnson stunned the home-state Bulldogs and signed with Clemson. Johnson, from LaGrange, announced he would attend Georgia during a press conference forty-eight hours before signing day. Two days later, he created shockwaves in the Peach and Palmetto states by signing with the Tigers.

The surprise addition of Johnson was the product of dogged persistence by Clemson assistants Jack Crowe and Tommy West, who continued to court Johnson after he announced for Georgia. Ford was never optimistic about landing Johnson because he knew the difficulty of swiping the top recruit in Georgia from the clutches of the Bulldogs. Seven years earlier, Ford and his staff got their hopes up about landing blockbuster running back Herschel Walker. He ended up signing with the Bulldogs after a lengthy, draining recruiting battle among Georgia, Clemson and others.

The night before signing day 1987, Ford began receiving angry calls from Georgia's staff. The Bulldogs' coaches couldn't locate Johnson, and they suspected Clemson's coaches might be up to something. Johnson had left home and was staying at the home of a friend. Crowe and West had turned him, and both later admitted they tried to hide him from the Bulldogs during that crucial period.

Georgia coach Vince Dooley said on signing day that he was "surprised and disappointed" by Johnson's decision but offered no further comment. Days later, Dooley was calling for the imposition of a forty-eight-hour "dead period" before signing day to prevent last-minute sales pitches from coaches. The rule was passed by the NCAA, and thereafter it was known as the "Dooley Rule."

The signing class was highly regarded. Linebacker Doug Brewster left Athens to attend Clemson. Another major defensive target, Ed McDaniel of Batesburg-Leesville, made his decision at the last minute and chose the Tigers. Ford was also excited about a freshman linebacker from Lamar named Levon Kirkland.

In June 1987, the NCAA discussed reducing coaching staffs, limiting scholarships and the length of playing seasons and capping the revenues a school could generate from its athletics program. Radical reform was deemed imperative to put a stop to what was termed "a spreading morass of recruiting, drug and academic scandals," according to an AP story. In February 1987, the NCAA slammed Southern Methodist's football program with the "death penalty" for repeated instances of major violations. The Mustangs, who had amassed a 41-5-5 record from 1981 to 1984, didn't play football in 1987 and 1988.

Clemson lost three major offensive weapons from the 1986 team with the departure of Kenny Flowers, Terrence Flagler and Terrance Roulhac, but everyone returned on the offensive line and that's what excited Ford.

Rodney Williams was back for his junior season at quarterback. The running back position had potential with Wesley McFadden and redshirt freshman Terry Allen. Fullbacks Tracy Johnson and Chris Lancaster were back, as was receiver Keith Jennings. Wideout Gary Cooper was a major surprise during spring practice. The defense, highlighted by powerful

Ford commends his players after a touchdown in the 1987 or 1988 season. After mediocrity in 1984, 1985 and part of 1986, Clemson was again a powerful program in Ford's last three years. *Courtesy of Clemson University Sports Information Department.*

linemen Michael Dean Perry and Raymond Chavous, returned eight starters from a group that allowed 104 rushing yards per game in 1986.

Perry, younger brother of William "the Refrigerator" Perry, was a fast talker who could back up his words with an extraordinary blend of strength and quickness. During the Tigers' second stadium scrimmage of August camp, Ford told Perry to hit the showers with ten minutes left in the first half. Perry had already totaled ten tackles, six of them for loss, and two sacks. Perry would go on to earn ACC player of the year honors, three years after his brother achieved the same distinction.

College & Pro Football Weekly picked Clemson number one before the season, as did the Atlanta *Constitution.* Famous oddsmaker Danny Sheridan gave his bowl predictions before the season and pegged the Tigers to play Oklahoma in the Orange Bowl.

Ford, at the time the only coach in ACC history to have compiled a career winning percentage exceeding 70 percent, was typically cautious about the lofty expectations. It was just three years earlier, after all, that his 1984 team finished the season with seven wins after starting it a presumed contender for the national title. But Ford acknowledged that this team "could be the best looking group in our nine years at Clemson."

The week of the opener against Western Carolina, Ford told reporters he wanted a fast start to the season. He pointed out that his first eight teams had compiled a 15-9 record in September and a 27-5 record in October. The previous season had begun with a deflating home loss to Virginia Tech.

Clemson rolled to an easy 43-0 win over Western Carolina, inserting its backups halfway through the third quarter. The next game took the Tigers to Virginia Tech to face the team that talked a bunch of trash and backed it up on the Tigers' home field in 1986.

The Hokies were in their first year under coach Frank Beamer, who returned to lead his alma mater after a stint at Murray State. This game would be Beamer's debut, and Ford said at his Tuesday press conference that Clemson's staff was in the dark as to the Hokies' intentions.

Clemson left no doubt on a rainy, muddy day in Blacksburg. The Tigers' 22-10 win was fueled by a stifling defensive effort that limited Virginia Tech to sixty yards of offense, the fewest by a Clemson opponent since 1963. Perry had three sacks and his first career interception. John Johnson was productive in the second game of his college career, starting at "bandit" end.

McFadden amassed 226 yards rushing and two touchdowns, including an 89-yard touchdown jaunt in the fourth quarter. The Hokies' lone touchdown came on a kickoff return.

"We were going against a great football team," Beamer said after the game. "Clemson is huge and quick and very talented."

Ranked number eight, Clemson had an opportunity to burnish its championship credentials the next week in a showdown with number eighteen Georgia at Death Valley. The border war between these two rivals, traditionally dominated by the Bulldogs, had grown into a must-see spectacle. The previous ten meetings had been decided by an average of 5.1 points, and Clemson's pulsating 31-28 win the previous year in Athens made the record over those ten games 5-4-1 in Georgia's favor.

The rivalry would be interrupted in 1988 and 1989 at Georgia's request as a result of the SEC's decision to increase its conference schedule to seven games. The Bulldogs preferred to alternate between Clemson and South Carolina every two years, and an end of an era was lamented by fans of the Tigers and Bulldogs.

Georgia running back Lars Tate added spice to the game-week buildup when he told the *Greenville News* that Clemson shouldn't put up much resistance to the Bulldogs. Tate was leading the nation in rushing with 175 yards per game, but Clemson was allowing a microscopic 16.5 yards per game on the ground.

"We can move the ball," Tate said. "They're not a super team or anything. They can be beat. We're not going to bow down to them."

Another storyline entering the game was Allen, the Tigers' young second-string tailback from Commerce, Georgia. Georgia expressed interest in Allen during the recruiting process but wanted him to play defensive back. Allen crossed the Bulldogs off his list and picked the Tigers because they promised him an opportunity to run the ball.

Dooley was asked about Allen at his press conference several days before the game at Clemson. "I don't know enough about Terry Allen to make a comment," he said. Dooley was asked if Georgia recruited Allen. He paused five seconds before saying, "No."

After Thursday's practice, Ford stood before his team and held up a pair of orange pants that were worn in the Tigers' Orange Bowl victory over Nebraska in the 1981 national championship season.

"You aren't going to wear them," Ford told his team.

The orange pants were reserved for special games, and to this point, Clemson had suffered just one loss in them since 1981. So there was some disappointment when the players heard they wouldn't be wearing them against the Bulldogs.

But then Ford dropped his sweatpants to reveal a pair of shiny new orange pants with thick stripes on the outside.

"But you are going to wear these," he told the team.

The Tigers' sacred orange britches had undergone a slick makeover, and their debut would come Saturday afternoon in front of the CBS cameras. The players closed the week's practice on an emotional high.

Two days later, Ford was frustrated for much of a wet, overcast afternoon at Death Valley. With six minutes left and the Tigers down 20-16, the visions of a national title were withering away when Ford elected to punt. Rusty Seyle's kick hit inside the five and bounced toward the end zone. Chinedu Ohan batted the ball backward as he fell into the end zone, then Johnson downed it to put Georgia inches from the goal line.

Quarterback James Jackson ran a sneak on first down and barely avoided a safety. On second down, Jackson rolled left on a designed run. Clemson brought immediate pressure up the middle, and the blockers were overwhelmed. Defensive back James Lott avoided a block attempt by Tate on the outside and reached Jackson in the end zone. Gene Beasley also stormed in, and linebacker Vince Taylor finally brought him down for a safety that unleashed an avalanche of noise from the capacity crowd. Suddenly, the Tigers were down just 20-18. They were getting the ball back, and all they needed was a field goal to win.

Donnell Woolford returned the free kick to the Clemson forty, and the Tigers' offense sprang to life when it had to. Allen ran like a man possessed against his home-state team, dashing for a big run early in the drive.

On third-and-seven from Georgia's thirty, Ford called option left and Williams was almost dropped for a loss that would've put the Tigers out of David Treadwell's field goal range. Williams barely got off the pitch, and then Allen made a spectacular run by avoiding two tacklers and then weaving across the field to the right for a huge gain that put the ball at the twelve-yard line.

Ford had burned the Tigers' timeouts in the third quarter as a result of miscommunication and disorganization on offense. The coach stared nervously at the clock as Treadwell, who'd missed a forty-one-yard attempt earlier in the fourth quarter, huddled with the field goal team on the field. Two ticks were left when the ball sailed through the uprights, giving Clemson a 21-20 triumph.

The 165-pound Treadwell, who'd never even played high school football before walking on to Clemson's football team in 1984, had never missed a field goal in the final eight minutes of a game. The year before, his forty-six-yard kick gave the Tigers their dramatic win in Athens. His reputation for making game-winning kicks earned him a nickname: "Fatal Attraction." He would earn first-team all-American honors in 1987.

Dooley was crestfallen after the game and took all the blame for calling the play that resulted in the game-turning safety. Nine of eleven games between Georgia and Clemson had been decided by seven points or less.

Ford speaks with kicker David Treadwell, a former walk-on who became an All-American thanks to a long line of game-winning kicks. *Courtesy of Clemson University Sports Information Department.*

"It was a dumb play on my part to even think about it," Dooley told reporters. "They hadn't scored a touchdown in a long time. We should have played it safe, punted out and let them take their chances trying to score a touchdown. I really feel bad about it. I don't know if I've ever felt as bad personally about losing a football game for a team that played as hard as we did. But it was all my fault."

Fans were talking Orange Bowl as they filed out of Death Valley that day. *Sports Illustrated* asked its readers to find anyone remaining on the Tigers' schedule that could beat them. Their next five games were at home, and a November 21 trip to South Carolina was considered the only daunting obstacle remaining.

The Tigers easily dispatched a bad Georgia Tech team the next week by a 33-12 score. Woolford, a junior defensive back, had a seventy-eight-yard punt return for a touchdown, Clemson's first punt return for a touchdown in seventeen years. Joe Henderson took a kickoff return ninety-five yards for a touchdown, ending Clemson's twenty-five-year streak of kickoffs without a touchdown. The offense sputtered some, though. Rodney Williams lost a fumble, and fans booed when he missed a wide-open receiver in the end zone.

Georgia Tech coach Bobby Ross said Clemson was "every bit as good as people say they are."

Clemson's fan base was buzzing at the thought of another national title with the Tigers 4-0 and ranked number eight heading into an open date. Some fans even did the unthinkable by pulling for rival South Carolina against Nebraska, theorizing that a more highly regarded Gamecocks team would boost Clemson's strength of schedule.

The open date allowed for the mending of some injuries, and the offense came up big in a 38-21 win over Virginia. The Tigers totaled 485 yards, 403 of them on the ground. Allen had 183 of those yards, McFadden 119. Ford was concerned about a sloppy defensive showing, though. The Cavaliers, 18-point underdogs, were down just 24-21 after driving for a touchdown on the first possession of the second half.

Duke came to Clemson the next week, and Ford was wary of an offense run by first-year head coach Steve Spurrier. The Blue Devils were off to a 3-2 start, which frustrated Spurrier enough to bench star quarterback Steve Slayden. Reserve Anthony Dilweg was listed as the starter entering the game against the Tigers.

"It doesn't matter if it's Slayden or the other youngster, Dunwiddy, Dalewitty or whatever," Ford said at his Tuesday press conference. "I hope I don't learn (Dilweg's name) very well."

Clemson sweated out a 17-10 win, securing the decisive points on an eleven-play, 97-yard drive capped by a 4-yard run by Tracy Johnson with 6:46 left. Duke outgained the Tigers 328-315, and Clemson's ten-game streak of 200-yard rushing games ended with a 183-yard day. Dilweg completed twenty-three of fifty passes for 305 yards.

A sign in the crowd during the Duke game read: "Hit Me Rodney, I'm Open." The attendance was ten thousand short of capacity, a strange sight given the presence of a Top Ten, undefeated team.

The next week, Clemson's faculty and student senates passed resolutions supporting IPTAY's plans for a new learning center for athletes. The proposed budget was $1.9 million, and IPTAY would foot the bill.

Clemson was ranked number seven and 6-0, but the mood was glum heading into a visit from N.C. State. On his weekly TV show, Ford called the Duke game "the worst exhibition of college football I've ever seen. Uninspired, unimaginative, pathetic." Tim Ellerbe, columnist for the *Independent-Mail* of Anderson, wrote that "Clemson paranoia" was permeating the fan base.

"Winning is no longer enough. Those fans want Clemson to beat people like Oklahoma's beating people. Clemson isn't."

Concern turned to outright despair after a complete first-half collapse against the Wolfpack. A team that entered as a 19-point underdog took a staggering, stunning lead of 30-0, and thousands of fans poured into the parking lots at halftime.

A valiant rally, fueled by a splendid passing performance from Williams, fell just short. Clemson pulled within 30-28 and had the ball in State territory with less than two minutes remaining, but Williams threw behind Johnson on fourth-and-five to end it. The Wolfpack finished the season 4-7.

Fans had spent weeks calling for sophomore backup Chris Morocco to replace Williams, and Morocco rose to the top spot after Williams suffered a knee injury two days after the N.C. State defeat. Morocco played well early against Wake Forest as the Tigers took a 10-0 lead, but he made a few bad mistakes late in the first half to help the Deacons take a 17-10 halftime lead in Death Valley. Williams returned in the second half, and the Tigers took control by going back to power football on the way to a 31-17 win in their orange pants.

Clemson was back in the Top Ten with a 7-1 record when it took to the road for a big ACC matchup at North Carolina. The Tar Heels had battled their way back into the conference race with wins over N.C. State and Maryland, and a portable lighting system was installed at Kenan Stadium to accommodate ESPN's 4:00 p.m. broadcast.

Tar Heels coach Dick Crum gushed about the Tigers a few days before the game.

"This might be the most complete Clemson team I've seen since I've been at Carolina," said Crum, who was facing considerable heat from North Carolina backers. "Danny and his staff have put together a potent offense, an outstanding defense and a great kicking game. Overall, this just might be better than the Clemson team that won the national championship in 1981." Ford, whose team entered the game as a three-point favorite, didn't agree with Crum's assessment.

North Carolina had been mediocre for several years, but Clemson still despised the Tar Heels. Before the game, players were greeted with a message taped to each locker in baby-blue ink: "This is Carolina Blue. Look at it closely. Hate it. Despise it. Beat it."

Clemson fulfilled the order when Treadwell kicked a thirty-yard field goal with thirty-two seconds left for a 13-10 victory that gave the Tigers a share of the ACC title. The offense sucked the life out of the Tar Heels with a nineteen-play drive in the final seven minutes, and Clemson beat North Carolina for the sixth time in seven years.

On fourth-and-two from North Carolina's thirty-eight with three minutes left, Ford called timeout and asked his players if they preferred to kick a field goal or go for the first down. They chose the latter, and Williams faked a handoff inside and pitched to Allen for a six-yard gain.

Crum, who took over the Tar Heels in 1978 and went through plenty of battles with Ford on and off the field, wouldn't survive his third five-win season in four years.

Clemson was two weeks away from a showdown in Columbia against a South Carolina team that was becoming dominant late in the season. Fans were abuzz over that game and possible bowl destinations, but a home date against Maryland was next and the Tigers had a chance to win the ACC outright.

The ACC took a dip in 1987, when Clemson was the conference's only team to appear in the AP poll the entire season. So winning the ACC wasn't as sexy as usual for Tiger fans. Charles Bennett of the *Independent-Mail* wrote that winning the ACC "rates in interest right up there with the latest taped replay of Australian rules football on ESPN…The Maryland game becomes significant in fans' eyes only if the Tigers lose."

But Clemson had beaten Maryland just four times in the previous fifteen meetings. Ford spent the week calling for his team to show a "killer instinct," and Clemson delivered in a 45-16 bloodletting. The all-orange Tigers rolled up 528 yards in winning their second straight conference title, and Rodney Williams played a flawless game both running the option and throwing. Clemson's players puffed victory cigars in the locker room, and Michael Dean Perry told reporters: "How sweet it is, gentlemen, how sweet it is. It's just like Maryland—up in smoke."

Maryland coach Joe Krivak didn't try to sugarcoat the spanking in his postgame presser.

"We just got our butts whipped. It was a good, old-fashioned, knockdown, drag-out tail whipping. They were by far the best team on the field today and they just whipped us. We're pretty battered and bruised up right now. It looked like Dinkirk Beach out there."

Ford announced after the game that he was barring his players and coaches from media interviews the next week. Perry, who sat out the Maryland game to heal a rib injury, held court with the press after the game and gave out his phone number to reporters who wanted quotes from him the next week. Perry, who grew up in Aiken and came close to signing with the Gamecocks, was jacked for the regular-season finale. Asked for his thoughts on the upcoming trip to Columbia, Perry responded with one word: "Dominance."

Ford's gag order didn't sit well with the media. In Charleston, Gene Sapakoff of the *News and Courier* called Ford the "Prince of Paranoia" and said he was treating his players "like a bunch of irresponsible children."

The Gamecocks were brimming with confidence, having smashed their previous five opponents by a combined score of 210-32. Included was a 48-0 dismemberment of the same N.C. State team that was up 30-0 on the Tigers after a half. South Carolina was ranked number twelve, four spots behind Clemson, but many observers believed the Gamecocks were playing as well as anyone. The Tigers were a seven-point underdog.

On Monday, press conference day in Columbia, South Carolina center Woody Myers said he heard Perry had been "talking a lot of trash up there in Clemson."

"I think our defensive line is going to give them hell," Myers said. "Their offensive line, I don't think they can handle it."

Sterling Sharpe, a star senior receiver for the Gamecocks, also responded to Perry's bold words. "I've seen a lot of teams that play their games in the papers, but it just doesn't look the same on the scoreboard."

A day later at his media gathering, Ford said the Gamecocks had the motivational edge. The previous year's game in Death Valley ended in a 21-21 tie after South Carolina missed a late field goal.

Ford walks the sidelines in a 1987 game at South Carolina. Clemson suffered a 20-7 loss in one of the most anticipated games of the storied rivalry's history. *Courtesy of Clemson University Sports Information Department.*

On a cold night in Columbia, the Gamecocks ambushed the Tigers 20-7 in a game televised nationally by ESPN. Clemson was missing Terry Allen because of a rib injury, but his presence might not have helped against a withering "Black Death" defense that held the Tigers to 166 yards.

Returning to his hometown, Williams was subjected to the most miserable night of his career after missing most of the week's practice with an injured knee. He spent the second half listening to deafening and derisive chants of his first name, and he tossed an interception for a touchdown late to end any remaining hope.

The Gamecocks had bludgeoned Virginia, N.C. State, Wake Forest and Clemson by a total of 156-17, and South Carolina players told the press afterward that they should be wearing Clemson's ACC championship rings.

Clemson fans were not happy to hear revelations that Ford condensed the offensive game plan as a result of Williams's injury. Kevin Kiley, ESPN's sideline reporter, noted during the broadcast that the Tigers had just eight running plays in their package for the game.

The scoreboard that night at Williams-Brice Stadium read: "GATOR 20, CITRUS 7."

Ford was matched against a coaching giant in the Orlando-based Florida Citrus Bowl. Penn State coach Joe Paterno was a year removed from slaying juggernaut Miami for the national title, and the defensive tactics he devised to bottle up the Hurricanes' powerful offense in that game left many calling him a coaching genius.

Paterno was concerned about defending Clemson's option. Don McPherson and Syracuse used the option to carve up the Nittany Lions in a 48-21 rout earlier in the season.

"(Williams) is a very underrated quarterback," Paterno told reporters. "For people who just saw the South Carolina game and not the others, there's a tendency to underestimate him."

Clemson fans rolled their eyes at this observation, still miffed about Williams' showing against the Gamecocks. *Blue-White Illustrated*, a Penn State fan publication, labeled the matchup "The Bowl Game That Time Forgot," alluding to the conservative styles of both teams.

Penn State entered the game without star running back Blair Thomas, who suffered a knee injury during a December workout. Thomas had

Ford poses with Joe Paterno before the Citrus Bowl in the 1987 season. Clemson throttled Paterno's Penn State team 35-10. *Courtesy of Clemson University Sports Information Department.*

rushed for 1,414 yards in 1987 and was considered an early frontrunner for the 1988 Heisman Trophy.

Ford had already beaten Woody Hayes and Tom Osborne in bowl games earlier in his tenure, and another big name went down hard when Clemson smoked Paterno's team 35-10 to hand the Nittany Lions their worst defeat in bowl history.

Williams achieved redemption, earning bowl MVP honors after completing fifteen of twenty-four passes for 214 yards. He also bagged his twenty-second win as a starter, more victories than any other quarterback in school history. The estimated fifteen thousand Clemson fans in attendance chanted his name with joy after he helped the offense amass 499 yards.

"That kid can throw the football," Paterno said after the game. "He's a good football player."

Ford said his offensive assistants talked him into a pass-heavy approach the morning of the game. Penn State ganged up against the run and was caught off guard by the Tigers' three-receiver sets and frequent first-down passes.

The Tigers didn't challenge for the national title, and they were humiliated in Columbia. But the decisive bowl victory, coupled with LSU's surprising 30-13 trouncing of the Gamecocks in the Gator Bowl, left fans feeling much better about things as they drove up I-95 in Florida.

The 1987 team became just the fourth in school history to win ten games. With a mere five starters departing, more success was on the way.

Chapter 11

1988

As Danny Ford reflected on a ten-win 1987 season, he called it his second-best Clemson team behind the 1981 squad that won the national title.

Ford was losing some major pieces including Michael Dean Perry, David Treadwell, John Phillips and Tony Stephens. But there was no reason to think the Tigers would slip from prominence, and a national title was deemed a realistic goal.

The offseason optimism was bolstered by the addition of a blockbuster recruiting class that included linebacker Wayne Simmons, defensive back Dexter Davis, defensive lineman Chester McGlockton and a celebrated quarterback from Louisiana named Michael Carr.

Ford turned forty on April 2, the day of Clemson's spring game. He moved into the summer comfortable with his returning starters, but a bit uneasy about the Tigers' depth.

Ten starters were returning on offense and eight on defense. Rodney Williams was back for his senior season and already owned the record for career wins by a quarterback. After watching Williams light up Penn State through the air in a 35-10 Florida Citrus Bowl victory, fans spent the offseason clamoring for the offense to pass the ball more in 1988.

Ford did not discourage talk of a national title as the season approached.

"It's not a bad question to have to answer when someone asks you if you can win the national championship," he told a gathering of ACC reporters over the summer. "We would like to have the best program we can have for our football players and our fans. Just so we don't get too carried away; we've got some of the biggest diehard fans you can have. I mean, I think that's why you play. We've won it one time at Clemson in about one hundred years. So it would be a pretty good deal to do it twice within six, eight or nine years."

Down the road in Columbia, Clemson's chief rival was going through a tumultuous offseason. In February, star receiver Ryan Bethea was arrested for possession of drugs with intent to distribute. Athletics director Bob Marcum was fired upon discovery of no drug-testing program for his athletes. His replacement, Dick Bestwick, was hired to clean things up but resigned after six months on the job, citing health reasons. There was rampant speculation that Gamecocks coach Joe Morrison forced him out.

Florida State replaced Georgia on the Tigers' schedule, and the summer was dominated by hype about the Seminoles' visit to Death Valley in the third week of the season. Florida State was ranked number one in the preseason, Clemson number four.

Veteran fullback Chris Lancaster was lost in August after aggravating a neck injury he'd suffered in high school. Carr, who was expected to contend for backup quarterback duties, suffered a broken arm during a scrimmage and was thought to be lost for the season.

Ford was annoyed by the Seminoles hysteria because Clemson had to play Virginia Tech and Furman first. Two years before, the Hokies silenced Death Valley with a 20-14 opening victory.

Clemson came out throwing against Virginia Tech, but the "Air Danny" experiment didn't last long. Dropped passes on the first and third plays of the game provoked Ford to tell his assistants to start running the ball, and the Tigers didn't throw again until they were well ahead. Ford's team produced 261 rushing yards that day in a 40-7 victory, Terry Allen rushing for 83 and Joe Henderson supplying 75.

Later that night, on national television, Florida State suffered a 31-0 annihilation at number two Miami. The swaggering Seminoles, led by brash defensive back Deion Sanders, had loudly proclaimed themselves the top team in the land with a televised song entitled "The Seminoles Rap." Miami's players, coming off a national title in 1987, were seething and salivating to spring an ambush. Florida State advanced past midfield just three times against the Hurricanes. Five Miami defenders intercepted passes by Seminoles quarterbacks Chip Ferguson, Peter Tom Willis and Casey Weldon.

Miami was a feared, ruthless juggernaut under Jimmy Johnson, having defeated the preseason number one team five years in a row. The Hurricanes had won thirty-two consecutive regular season games and hadn't lost to Florida State since 1984. Clemson fans hoped their defense could pose similar problems for the Seminoles.

Ford did his best to build up Furman, which won the Division I-AA national title in 1986. But the Florida State questions from the media persisted.

"Who cares about Florida State?" he snapped at his Tuesday press conference. "We have got to go out and play like we did Saturday and improve or we're going to have a loss on our hands."

Ford was asked about the Tigers' number three ranking. Florida State had tumbled to number ten.

Ford meets with the media after a home game. Ford was known for his colorful, homespun quips during press conferences. *Courtesy of Clemson University Sports Information Department.*

"Polls are for holding up goal posts. They don't mean anything this time of year."

Clemson scaled down its offensive playbook against the Paladins and won 23-3. Afterward, Ford walked into the interview room and asked the reporters: "Who wants to talk about Florida State now?"

The Seminoles rebounded with a 49-13 pasting of Southern Mississippi, which would finish 10-2 led by sophomore quarterback Brett Favre. Bobby Bowden was still searching for his first national title, but he had built Florida State into a powerhouse by going on the road and slaying elite competition. By this point, his road record was 48-25-2, and it included high-profile victories in Ann Arbor, Lincoln, Baton Rouge and Auburn.

The clamor for tickets began in April and lasted all summer. Ticket manager Van Hilderbrand said demand was higher for this game than for any of the past visits from South Carolina or Georgia. Sports information director Bob Bradley said he hadn't fielded as many media requests for a game since Notre Dame's 1977 game at Death Valley.

Bowden was known for trick plays and audacious risk-taking, and Ford's staff knew the Seminoles were cooking up something special for this one. The week of the game, they received a tip that indicated that the Seminoles were installing an elaborate fake punt they'd never used before.

Sanders, then a senior, had played minor league baseball for the New York Yankees organization the previous summer. He bragged about wearing "five to seven thousand dollars" worth of gold chains around his neck, including one that held a pendant bearing the nickname he coined for himself: "PRIMETIME."

Sanders sneered when he arrived at the stadium and saw Clemson's game programs promoting Tigers defensive back Donnell Woolford for the Thorpe Award. Bowden started Ferguson, who was from nearby Spartanburg.

Clemson's team descended down the Hill to a soggy field in its treasured orange pants, and Florida State donned white pants for the first time in thirty years. They were a gift from famous alumnus Burt Reynolds, who paid fifty dollars per pair.

Ford stands at the top of the Hill before a 1988 game against Florida State. At his right side is Tigers basketball coach Cliff Ellis. *Courtesy of Clemson University Sports Information Department.*

In a game televised nationally by CBS, the Tigers took a 14-7 lead into halftime after Williams drove the offense ninety-nine yards on seventeen plays and scored on a seven-yard run.

Florida State took control in the third quarter. Sanders strutted onto the field for a punt return and screamed to Clemson's sideline that he was going to score a touchdown. He fielded the punt, made a few jukes and was off on a seventy-six-yard jaunt to the end zone. Clemson's student section hurled cups and mini bottles at Sanders as he kneeled to pray.

Soon thereafter, the Seminoles drove seventy-seven yards on five plays for a touchdown to take a 21-14 lead. Clemson later had to block a field goal to avoid falling into a 10-point hole.

With hopes slipping away, the Tigers drove sixty-six yards and pulled within 21-20 on a nineteen-yard run by Tracy Johnson with 2:32 left. Ford elected to kick the game-tying extra point as his assistants lobbied to go for two. He believed his defense would come up with a stop to create a chance at a game-winning field goal.

On second down, Clemson was presented with a gift-wrapped opportunity when Otis Moore pressured Ferguson, resulting in a pass that fluttered toward linebacker Vince Taylor at Florida State's twenty-four-yard line. Taylor could not hold on, and the ball fell incomplete.

The Seminoles couldn't convert on third down, and with 1:33 left, Bowden sent his punt team onto the field. Ford briefly considered burning a timeout to assure his players were prepared for a fake, but he elected to save it.

The ball was snapped and, while punter Tim Corlew leaped and flailed as if it was sailing over his head toward the Hill, was reaching the hands of the fullback and then being placed between the legs of upback LeRoy Butler. Butler froze for the briefest instant as the other Seminoles spilled to the right side of the field, taking orange-clad Tigers with them like a magnet.

It was now obvious that the play was a fake, but almost everyone in attendance—including CBS cameras—was fooled. The left side was wide open for Butler, who was instructed to freeze for 3 seconds before bursting away. He later said he took off at 1.5 seconds after hearing someone yelling for him to go.

This was Butler's postgame recollection of his first few steps: "A few of them touched me, but they didn't know I had the ball."

Butler dashed seventy-eight yards before Woolford forced him out at the one-yard line. It would be forever known as the "Puntrooskie," one of the most famous plays in college football history—at Clemson's expense, and with the stakes sky-high.

Ford after the game: "It was a nice call. It was a good gamble and very successful. We knew they had it, but I'm not sure if our people were warned about it this particular time."

Ford is interviewed by CBS sideline reporter Pat O'Brien moments after his team fell to Florida State on the famed "Puntrooskie" call by Seminoles coach Bobby Bowden. *Courtesy of Clemson University Sports Information Department.*

Bowden after the game: "We put it in this week because I thought we might need it. They chased all the motion to the right…If we miss it, they're going to hit a field goal and win. I just wanted somebody to win the game."

The Seminoles still had to score the decisive points. On first-and-goal, Florida State botched the handoff and lost two yards. Before the next play, the twenty-five-second clock expired as the Seminoles tried to call a timeout they didn't have. Confusion reigned, and Ford demanded an explanation. No penalty was called, the clock was stopped and Richie Andrews was summoned to kick the game-winning field goal with thirty-two seconds left.

Ken Burger of the *News and Courier* of Charleston wrote: "It was just one of those days when the Tiger Rag sagged, the referees gagged and believing just wasn't enough."

Two days later, Ford was still steamed about the officiating when he spoke at the Atlanta Touchdown Club. He called one of the ACC refs who worked the Florida State game "an idiot" for failing to recognize a Seminoles' fumble in the third quarter. Clemson recovered the ball, but the runner was ruled down and Florida State scored a touchdown two plays later.

A reporter from an Atlanta newspaper attended the speaking engagement, and Ford's rant was big news the next day.

> *They throw a pass over the middle, he's hit. Complete fumble, complete fumble. I got a guy that's 23 yards away, out of position, that calls the ball dead. I got an umpire on the film going, "Clemson's ball." I got another idiot from my conference, 23 yards away, running in and saying it was dead. And I asked the official on my sideline who made the call that the ball was down, and he said, "Both of us." He said he came in and couldn't see the play, so he saw the other official, and he pointed down.*

The Tigers went to Atlanta the next week and drubbed a bad Georgia Tech team 30-13. A sixty-eight-yard interception return for a touchdown by linebacker Doug Brewster broke open the game, and the Yellow Jackets' losing streak against I-A teams stretched to thirteen games.

Clemson had an open date the next week, and the ACC's coordinator of officials released a statement acknowledging "some officiating errors" in the loss to Florida State. Conference commissioner Gene Corrigan reminded Ford that coaches were not supposed to comment publicly on officiating. Ford said he wasn't aware of such a policy.

A trip to Virginia was next, and the Cavaliers had become formidable under George Welsh. The Tigers were trying to improve to 28-0 all-time in the series, and Ford said the week of the game that the streak would end someday.

"I sure hope I'm not here when it does," he said.

Clemson survived in Charlottesville after Williams tossed a fourteen-yard touchdown pass to Chip Davis with 1:52 left, giving the Tigers a 10-7 victory. The Cavaliers had gone up 7-3 when Shawn Moore connected with Herman Moore for a fourteen-yard touchdown pass with 5:27 on the clock. Williams extended his streak of pass attempts without an interception to 104. Ford, whose team lost three fumbles, said the Tigers "dodged a bullet."

The next week, Ford was bothered that his team hadn't yet dominated anyone. Domination seemed unlikely against Duke, a team that brought a 5-0 record into Death Valley. In their second year under Steve Spurrier, the Blue Devils were ranked sixth nationally in total offense. ESPN canceled plans to show Alabama-Tennessee in favor of this matchup.

The Tigers made their coach a happy man with a 49-17 gutting of Spurrier's team, pressuring quarterback Anthony Dilweg constantly and intercepting four of his passes.

Clemson's offense hummed for 533 yards, 388 of them on the ground. Terry Allen had 134 yards on seventeen carries. Veteran defensive back James Lott after the game: "The main thing we did today is make a statement for the rest of the year."

Next was a trip to N.C. State, led by third-year coach Dick Sheridan. The Wolfpack had smoked the Tigers 27-3 in 1986, and in 1987, they rolled into Death Valley and shockingly built a 30-0 lead before holding on for a two-point win.

State boasted a stingy defense that had not allowed a touchdown in twenty-one of twenty-four quarters, including twelve in a row. The Wolfpack was ranked first nationally in total defense (210 yards per game), first in scoring defense (8.5 points per game) and second in rushing defense (75.7 yards per game). Clemson failed to reach the end zone in a 10-3 defeat, and for the first time as a head coach, Ford had suffered three consecutive losses to one team. Williams had a bad game, throwing three interceptions after having gone 122 straight attempts without one. He missed Stacy Fields on a deep ball, badly overthrowing him on a play that would've been a touchdown. He hit an official squarely in the head on another pass. He also had two bad pitches that resulted in lost yardage on two third-down plays.

Chris Gardocki missed two second-quarter field-goal attempts, both from forty yards. The Tigers' day was summed up with three minutes left, when Gary Cooper took an end-around from Williams and found plenty of room on the left side. What looked like a long touchdown run turned into a minimal gain when offensive lineman Jeb Flesch veered into Cooper's path and tripped him up.

The Tigers fell out of the ACC lead at 5-2 overall and 3-1 in the conference, and some fans were calling for Chris Morocco or DeChane Cameron to replace Williams.

As the team was preparing for a game at Wake Forest, injured quarterback Michael Carr told the *Times-Picayune* of New Orleans he was considering transferring because of homesickness. Carr, from Amite, Louisiana, was deemed the jewel of the 1988 recruiting class. He'd suffered a broken arm two weeks into August practice and hadn't played since.

Clemson left Winston-Salem with a 38-21 victory over Wake Forest, and Maryland's last-second win at North Carolina put the Tigers into a three-way tie for the ACC lead. The offense rebounded with a 447-yard day against the Deacons, including 349 rushing. Allen contributed 154 yards and had a 63-yard touchdown run in the third quarter.

Williams responded to the criticism by passing for ninety-eight yards and rushing for fifty-four, including touchdown runs of seventeen and one yard. "I expect him to play like that every football game," Ford told reporters after the game. "We don't expect him to play bad."

The Tigers, who dropped two spots to number seventeen in the AP poll, were heavy favorites when they returned home to face a bad North Carolina team. The Tar Heels were 1-7 under first-year coach Mack Brown.

The rivalry with North Carolina was white-hot from 1980 to 1985, when the games between the two were decided by an average of 5.3 points. The two programs had gone in opposite directions in recent years, and Clemson encountered little resistance on this day in a 37-14 pasting. The Tigers totaled 500 yards of offense, 336 on the ground, and never punted.

A third consecutive ACC title was at stake when Clemson went to College Park the next week to play a mediocre Maryland team. The Tigers found themselves down 14-13 at halftime but took control with a big third quarter that featured two long touchdown drives. Clemson pounded Maryland 49-25, totaling 373 rushing yards and again going without a punt.

Allen surpassed one thousand yards on the season and became the first runner in Clemson history to reach two thousand career yards as a sophomore. When Ford recruited Allen, he told him he could play tailback for a year and then move to the secondary. Allen was blossoming into one of the elite tailbacks in college football.

The Tigers had zero problems shifting from a third consecutive ACC title to a visit from South Carolina in the regular-season finale. If the 20-7 beating they absorbed the previous year in Columbia wasn't enough, Gamecocks defensive end Kevin Hendrix stoked them even more by popping off as rivalry week began.

Hendrix said IPTAY stood for "I Pick Taters All Year." He took aim on Williams, who had suffered through a miserable night the year before in Columbia against the Gamecocks' powerful defense.

"The only thing I see is that when I watch him on film he always tries to primp around back there in the backfield and act cool. I mean, he tries to primp like some black guy would or something and I think that kind of sets the tone for what kind of person he really is."

The words were coming from a member of a team that had tumbled disastrously after a 6-0 start and Top Ten ranking. The Gamecocks suffered a 34-0 loss at Georgia Tech, a team that had lost fifteen straight games to Division I-A teams. Florida State rolled through Columbia and tattooed them with a 59-0 humiliation on national television. And the week before their trip to Clemson, the Gamecocks struggled to get by a bad Navy team.

And on top of all that, South Carolina was dealing with a steroid scandal that rocked the football program and heaped scrutiny on sixth-year coach Joe Morrison. He'd delivered some of the finest moments in the Gamecocks' history, and the 1987 demolition of the Tigers signaled that Clemson's in-state supremacy could be coming to an end. In reality, South Carolina's program was sinking.

Ford allowed his players to participate in media interviews the week of the game, going away from the gag order he imposed the previous year before the Tigers' loss in Columbia. Williams refused to get into the war of words with Hendrix, telling reporters "everybody's got their opinion."

Williams did say the Tigers hadn't taken the rivalry game as seriously as the Gamecocks had in recent years, contributing to a 21-21 tie in 1986 and the embarrassing loss the previous season. He said his team seemed more content with ACC titles and big bowl games those years, but he was determined to change that in his last shot at South Carolina.

Ford won four of his first five over the Gamecocks from 1979 to 1983, but from that point to 1988 his only victory in the rivalry came in 1985. He told his players to approach this game like it was "the biggest of their entire lives."

Asked by a reporter if he'd rather beat South Carolina or win a bowl game over Oklahoma, Ford responded: "I think for the importance of our community, our state, my health and my job that this one would probably be very important."

The game's importance to Ford diminished considerably late in the week when his mother suffered a heart attack, the third such episode over a three-week period. As of Friday evening, Ford wasn't certain whether he'd coach the game or return to his home of Gadsden, Alabama, and be with his mother. Her condition had improved by Saturday morning. Ford decided to coach the game and promised his mother a victory over the Gamecocks.

Defensive tackle Richard McCullough devoted the pre-game prayer to Ford's mother, and the Tigers played inspired football on an overcast afternoon in taking a 16-0 lead. The Gamecocks' first three possessions ended in fumbles, and linebacker Jesse Hatcher caused two of them.

South Carolina scored a touchdown late in the first half to trim it to 16-7, and in the locker room Ford informed the team of his promise to his mother. The Tigers pulled away in the second half for a 29-10 win, and Williams closed his final home game in style by scoring a late touchdown and sparking adoring chants of his first name—a sharp contrast from the scene a year earlier in Columbia, when Williams endured derisive howls of his name by Gamecocks fans.

Clemson accepted a bid to the Florida Citrus Bowl to play Oklahoma. South Carolina settled for a trip to Memphis to face Indiana in the Liberty Bowl. The Tigers made a resounding statement that they were no longer in the Gamecocks' shadow. Ford accepted the state championship trophy from a South Carolina assistant and said: "Come on back home, boy."

"I'd like to think they just had a couple of good years and now we're back to dominating," receiver Ricardo Hooper said in the Anderson *Independent-Mail*.

Ford to reporters: "We've let some tradition slip away from Clemson against South Carolina, I think. We needed to start something."

Ken Burger, sports columnist at the *News and Courier* of Charleston, penned a pointed contrast between the two programs.

> *They are 8-3 and going to a bowl game. But they are zombies. They are dead…Somewhere, somebody must be wondering what Gamecock football is all about. If it's making money and building beautiful facades, then it's a success. If it's to become a national power and strike fear in the hearts of major programs around the nation, it's a failure. And the most frustrating part of it for Gamecock fans has to be that Clemson has done both.*

Oklahoma had played Miami for the national title in 1987, but the Sooners' program was a wreck heading into the bowl matchup with the Tigers. The NCAA had socked Barry Switzer's team with three years of probation for recruiting violations. Starting quarterback Charles Thompson had suffered a broken leg early in the Sooners' 7-3 loss to Nebraska in the regular-season finale. And Oklahoma's players trashed an entire floor of the team hotel soon after their arrival in Orlando.

Clemson had been working out in Florida since December 18, and Switzer expressed concern that his team might be out of shape after taking off for two weeks. The Tigers were a slight favorite over the 9-2 Sooners, and Ford said his team had to play "better than our best" to win.

The Sooners were talking trash in the days leading up to the game. Defensive back Kevin Thompson told reporters that Oklahoma was "going to show the NCAA that they put the best team in the country on probation." Another defensive back, Scott Garl, said he had seen better backs than Terry Allen. "If we hold Clemson to seven points like we did Nebraska, we'll beat their ass," Garl said.

Oklahoma's powerful wishbone offense averaged 343 rushing yards a game during the season but produced less than 100 yards through three quarters against the Tigers. Clemson held on for a 13-6 win after Dexter Davis batted down a pass in the end zone.

Switzer was far from a gracious loser after the game, saying Clemson approached the bowl "like it was a national championship game" by arriving early in Florida. "When we go to a bowl as a loser of our

Ford and Oklahoma coach Barry Switzer speak before their teams meet in the Citrus Bowl during the 1988 season. It turned out to be Switzer's last game as the Sooners' coach. *Courtesy of Clemson University Sports Information Department.*

conference, we're going to leave on Christmas day, just like we always have, because the game isn't nationally significant to us," he said.

Ford had guided Clemson to its second consecutive 10-win season, but Switzer didn't seem impressed. "Clemson would have to go 71-1 and win four national championships to equal what we have accomplished."

Ford, who did not hear Switzer's diatribe, was next on the podium. As the two coaches crossed paths Ford told Switzer: "Thank you, buddy." Ford added another big name to his growing list of bowl-game conquests—Hayes, Osborne, Paterno and now Switzer. It ended up being Switzer's last game as Oklahoma's coach. "We had a lot to prove today," Ford told reporters. "You can put Oklahoma in that bag now."

Ford went on to say that the victory showed that the ACC "can do more than shoot basketballs." Oklahoma had previously gone 16-0 all-time against the ACC. "It also shows Clemson has come a long way in football," Ford said.

The coach campaigned for sports writers to put his team in the Top Ten. The Tigers rose four spots to number nine, their first Top Ten finish in the AP poll since 1982. "The 1980s have been pretty good to little old Clemson University," Ford said that day in Orlando.

Soon thereafter, Ford reviewed the 1988 season with a reporter from the *State* and answered a question about the importance of image.

"It used to matter," he said. "It doesn't anymore...I'm not into any university's personality. I'm into winning football games."

Chapter 12

1989

Clemson's football program moved into 1989 having lost the most lettermen in school history (thirty-three) and thirteen starters from a team that finished with ten wins and a Top Ten ranking.

The 1988 team had twenty-eight seniors, and the departure of a number of key figures meant Danny Ford's program was undergoing a makeover. But there was still plenty of momentum, still reason to think the Tigers could remain a national power in Ford's eleventh season.

Ford signed a blockbuster recruiting class, one he called "the most national recruiting class we've had since I've been at Clemson." It was highlighted by defensive lineman Brentson Buckner of Georgia, running back Rodney Blunt of Florida, defensive back James Trapp of Oklahoma and quarterback Richard Moncrief of Alabama.

The offseason was marked by two tragedies that profoundly affected Ford. A little more than a week after Ford spontaneously dropped by the office of Joe Morrison in Columbia for an informal chat before an IPTAY function, Morrison collapsed while playing racquetball and died of a massive heart attack.

In six seasons as South Carolina's head coach, Morrison posed serious challenges to Clemson's Palmetto State supremacy. But the coaches got along well off the field. On their last visit, they drank beer together in Morrison's office as the Gamecocks' coach relayed the pressures of NCAA and administrative scrutiny in the wake of the 1988 steroid scandal.

In May, Ford lost a much closer friend when former longtime assistant Tom Harper, fifty-six, died in a Savannah hotel room after speaking to an IPTAY gathering. Harper, a thirty-six-year coaching veteran who joined Ford before the national title season of 1981, had ended his coaching career months earlier by accepting a position as an administrative assistant to Ford. He was found with a book over his chest in his hotel room after suffering a heart attack. For years, he'd refused to take yearly physicals with the other Clemson coaches.

Also in this offseason, Ford began to publicize his festering grievances with his superiors at Clemson. In 1986, first-year university president Max Lennon nixed his idea for a new athletics dormitory. And now, three years later, Ford still wasn't getting his way. At a gathering of Clemson supporters in Columbia, Ford assailed the administration's plans to sink its money into a new learning center for athletes.

The Gamecocks were on the verge of moving into a plush new dorm, and Ford told supporters he was embarrassed to take recruits to twenty-seven-year-old Mauldin Hall. He called this "one of my unhappy moments at Clemson," and he encouraged IPTAY members to make their feelings known to the powers at the school. The *State* presented Ford's comments to athletics director Bobby Robinson, who said an athletics dorm had been "a dead issue for about two years."

Ford's 1988 recruiting class was highlighted by the signing of an athletic, strong-armed quarterback from Louisiana named Michael Carr, but by the summer of 1989, Carr had been nothing more than a headache for the football staff. Carr suffered a broken arm during August camp in 1988 and later became homesick, threatening to transfer to LSU. The drama continued after the season, and Ford put Carr off-limits to media interviews during 1989 spring practice.

Carr was one of five quarterbacks competing for the starting job vacated by Rodney Williams, who won twenty-eight games the previous three seasons. Ford told reporters that Carr "needs to decide whether he wants to be a football player here or not."

Clemson was trying to become the first team in ACC history to claim four consecutive conference titles, and ACC media picked the Tigers to pull off the feat. Ford said the votes were "out of courtesy more than anything else." There was strong sentiment from some that N.C. State and Virginia would eclipse the Tigers in 1989. At Clemson's fan appreciation day in August, junior tailback Terry Allen said his team was being treated like an underdog.

The typical preseason talk of polls and prognostications abruptly ended in late August when the *Constitution* of Atlanta reported that the NCAA was investigating Clemson for possible recruiting violations. Lennon immediately announced that the school would conduct its own investigation. The revelations consumed Clemson's community and fueled speculation that the football program might be slapped with the NCAA's "death penalty" if major violations were discovered so soon after the Tigers' probation from 1982 to 1984. SMU didn't field a team in 1987 and 1988 as a result of widespread major violations. Oklahoma's football program had been hammered by the NCAA, as had the basketball programs at Kentucky and Kansas. Clemson fans feared Ford's program might be next.

The *Constitution* reported that the NCAA had gathered information through interviews with former Clemson recruits who ended up at Auburn, North Carolina, South Carolina and Georgia. Charlie Lyle, the Gamecocks' former recruiting coordinator, told the *Independent-Mail* of Anderson that six to ten South Carolina players were interviewed by an NCAA investigator eighteen months before.

In early August, the NCAA visited Carr's hometown of Amite, Louisiana, and spoke with the mother of a close friend of Carr's. The mother told the *Times-Picayune* of New Orleans that Carr had begun wearing new clothes and driving a new car shortly after signing with Clemson. Carr's high school football coach told reporters Carr confirmed to him that Clemson broke NCAA rules while recruiting him. Carr's sister was quoted as saying the stories about recruiting violations involving her brother were "all lies."

Initial reports said Carr drew suspicion in his hometown when he came home for Christmas in 1988 driving a new Toyota Supra. But Carr's brother, a chemical engineer in Baton Rouge, told the *Greenville News* that he had purchased a used car for Carr a year-and-a-half before. Carr blamed his former high school coach for the NCAA scrutiny and accused him of lying out of hatred for Clemson. Carr abruptly left the team at one point during August camp but returned after a few days.

Arkansas assistant Jack Crowe, who served under Ford from 1986 to 1988, told reporters that the allegations were bogus and that the NCAA was out to get Clemson. The Tigers had signed players from fifteen states over the previous two recruiting classes.

"You've got to have a tough hide to walk into somebody's back yards and get players, because if you outwork people—and that's what you do in recruiting—you're going to be accused of cheating," Crowe told the *Independent-Mail*. "There are a significant number of rules today specifically to stop Danny. The non-work rules. The rules hurt the guy who wants to outwork somebody, the old established guys who work at it. That's got Danny Ford's name right on it."

On August 23, Clemson learned that it was under official investigation when the NCAA sent notice of a "preliminary inquiry." Lennon made an announcement urging faculty and staff to report any academic irregularities involving Clemson athletes.

Ford, who was not allowed to comment on the investigation, tried to focus on football as the opener with Furman approached. The biggest on-field storyline was the battle at quarterback between Chris Morocco and DeChane Cameron. Morocco had twenty-three games of experience and was considered the leader, but Ford said he never had a quarterback race as close as this one.

More negative headlines came several days before the opener when it was revealed that Allen had been arrested for driving under the influence. The Tigers' star tailback was suspended for the Furman game.

Morocco started as the number twelve Tigers defeated the Paladins 30-0. Cameron played regularly in the game and completed all six of his pass attempts.

Next for Clemson was a game that players and coaches had been thinking about all offseason. Florida State had come to Death Valley the previous year and won on the strength of Bobby Bowden's famous "Puntrooskie" call, and now the Tigers had another shot at the Seminoles in Tallahassee, Florida.

"I think Clemson is going to be as fired up to beat Florida State as any team we've ever played because of last year," Bowden told reporters the week of the game. "They physically beat us up last year. They had the game tied, and they were in position to win it when that thing happened. I imagine that hasn't sat too well."

Florida State had amassed a 22-2 record in 1987 and 1988, the only losses coming to Miami. So it was a jolt when Southern Miss pulled off a 30-26 upset of the Seminoles in Jacksonville, Florida, to open the season. The Golden Eagles were coached by Curley Hallman, a former Ford assistant, and quarterbacked by Brett Favre.

Ford engaged in his typical round of poor-mouthing during his Tuesday press luncheon, saying the Seminoles were "faster, quicker and more talented" than Clemson. But there was no question he was looking forward to the rematch.

"It's a different fair from last week," he said. "This isn't a county fair. This is a state fair. This is a big deal."

Ford orchestrated a stunt as the Tigers gathered for their last practice of the week. A graduate assistant dressed up as the Seminole mascot and rode a horse onto the field, planting a spear into the turf to mimic the pre-game ritual that would take place two days later in Tallahassee.

The Seminoles' ranking dropped from number six to sixteen after the Southern Miss upset. Clemson was ranked number ten, but few people thought the Tigers would leave Tallahassee with a win.

In a primetime matchup televised by ESPN, the Tigers weren't the least bit intimidated when they walked into Doak Campbell Stadium and saw all the trappings of a powerhouse program. They stunned the Seminoles, and perhaps even themselves, by roaring to a 21-0 lead in the second quarter.

Clemson totaled 148 yards before Florida State produced a first down. Wayne Simmons took an interception 73 yards for a touchdown, and Allen burst 73 yards for another score to help Clemson build a 28-10 lead by halftime. The estimated 7,500 orange-clad fans in attendance were giddy, turning Florida State's "FSU" chant into "0 and 2."

The Tigers held on in the second half for a 34-23 victory, and Ford said afterward that he didn't know if a Clemson team had ever played better. As he reflected on an offense that averaged a staggering 7.07 yards on just fifty-five plays, Ford pulled a chunk of sod from his pocket.

"We'll get a tombstone going tomorrow," he said, referring to a sod cemetery back home at Clemson that marked the Tigers' big road victories.

The next morning, Bowden gathered with reporters for breakfast and heaped praise on Ford and Clemson. Bowden's home record as Florida State's coach stood at 60-15-1.

"They came out there with a mission, right off the bat. They were of one accord in that regard. I have to hand it to Danny. He did a great job coming down here and taking complete charge. I mean he didn't waste a down taking charge...If Danny's kids don't get overconfident—and he does a pretty good job with that—they're going to be hard to beat."

For the third consecutive year, Clemson fans started fantasizing about a national title early in the season.

The number seven Tigers went to Virginia Tech and claimed a 27-7 victory the next week. Three days later, Ford said he was tired of answering questions about the quarterback situation. Morocco had played well at Florida State and seemed to have a strong hold on the job.

The Tigers were rolling right along at 4-0 after an easy win over Maryland, and no one saw an upset coming as they prepared for a trip to face 1-3 Duke. Blue Devils coach Steve Spurrier said going in that his team faced "hundred to one" odds of vanquishing Clemson. Ford was cautious, saying the game meant more to Duke than usual because the Tigers hadn't visited Wallace Wade Stadium since 1985. Ford and his staff were also distracted by the presence of NCAA investigators on Clemson's campus as they prepared for the Blue Devils.

An estimated 22,600 fans watched a mammoth 21-17 upset of the number seven Tigers on a wet day in Durham. Clemson went up 14-0 but watched its dream season disappear as Duke knocked off the Tigers for the first time since 1980, when Spurrier was offensive coordinator for a team that flattened Clemson in Death Valley.

A little-known running back named Randy Cuthbert exasperated Clemson fans by picking up large chunks of yards on the ground and also doing damage as a receiver. He rushed for as many yards against the Tigers (fifty-five) as he had in the previous four games. Clemson's players said they had never even seen Cuthbert on film.

Spurrier perplexed the Tigers' defensive staff with his second-half play-calling. The Devils pounded Cuthbert with the run when Clemson inserted an extra defensive back and took to the air when the Tigers loaded up against the run.

Wrote David Westin of the *Augusta Chronicle:* "Clemson defenders are still trying to figure out who that guy was in the No. 42 jersey."

Quarterback Billy Ray, a transfer from Alabama, threw for 262 yards and two touchdowns. He was intercepted five times, but the Tigers didn't convert any of the miscues into points. Clemson lost fumbles on two of the interception returns and racked up 88 yards in penalties.

The Tigers had 266 yards of offense in the first half and 95 thereafter. Ford looked back at the Florida State victory and said it produced a feeling among his players that they could win by merely showing up. The national title hopes were circling the drain.

The Tigers pronounced themselves back on track the next week when they beat Virginia 34-20 at Death Valley. The Cavaliers were a strong program at the time and would finish the 1989 season with ten wins and a Top Twenty ranking.

A visit from Georgia Tech was Clemson's next task, and the Tigers probably didn't feel the need to be all that concerned. They had destroyed the Yellow Jackets by a combined score of 90-28 the previous two years, and Georgia Tech entered as a 20-point underdog. The NCAA investigators were back on campus asking questions as the Tigers prepared for the game.

The previous Saturday, the Jackets snapped a sixteen-game ACC losing streak with a 28-24 victory over Maryland. In the locker room after that game, one player told reporters that Clemson would "get all they can handle."

By halftime, the fans at Death Valley sat in stunned silence trying to figure out how Georgia Tech was up 23-6. The Jackets went on to beat the Tigers 30-14, and Ford ripped his players after the game.

"We physically got beat. Not by accident, but by a better football team than we were. I just don't like anything we did. We got whipped. When you don't play football and they do, you ain't got no excuse. They literally wore us out."

Clemson's hopes of a fourth consecutive ACC title were on life support, and the same team that looked unstoppable in Tallahassee had plummeted out of the Top Twenty-five five weeks later. Ford said the landmark win over Florida State "fooled everybody, including ourselves."

The Tigers gathered their bearings for a visit from number twelve N.C. State and earned a 30-10 victory that was satisfying on a number of levels. Ford had lost to Dick Sheridan three straight years, and the Pack was atop the ACC standings with a 4-0 record. Clemson was an unranked underdog on its home field.

Ford, who informed his players during the pre-game meal that they'd wear orange pants for the Wolfpack, improved to 6-5 against N.C. State. A defense that had given up so many big plays to Georgia Tech allowed precious few to the Wolfpack. The Tigers improved to 15-2 in orange pants under Ford.

Ford surprised fans by inserting Michael Carr on kickoff returns. Carr had one return for twenty yards, but two other kickoffs sailed through the end zone.

Carr got some mop-up duty at quarterback in the next game, a 44-10 victory over Wake Forest. Morocco had a big first half and gave way to Cameron and Carr in the second half. Carr tossed an interception and said afterward that he was nervous.

Allen, who'd missed the previous two games with an injured knee, played briefly early against the Deacons but limped off the field and didn't return.

The Tigers had wrapped up their home schedule. They were 7-2 and ranked number twenty-one heading into their last two regular-season games against North Carolina and South Carolina.

The Tar Heels were headed for their second consecutive one-win season under Mack Brown, and Clemson used an overpowering third quarter to win 35-3. The Tigers had six sacks, linebacker Levon Kirkland had an interception that the offense converted into a quick touchdown and Joe Henderson ran for 163 yards on twenty-five carries.

After an open date, next was a trip to Columbia against a South Carolina team that had won six games under first-year coach Sparky Woods. The Gamecocks got off to a promising start in 1989 but slid after star quarterback Todd Ellis was lost to a season-ending injury.

Clemson was a 14-point favorite and had dominated South Carolina the year before in a 29-10 victory, so it appeared the rivalry was taking on its traditional orange-tinted glow. But Ford was taking nothing for granted. He still remembered the bitter taste of a 20-7 loss on his last trip to Columbia two years earlier, and he spent all week reminding his players of that experience.

Both teams were battered and bruised. Allen had been ailing with a knee injury for weeks, but he was determined to play after missing the 1987 game in Columbia with a rib injury.

ESPN chose to televise the game to the nation in primetime. Doug Nye of the *State* called network executive Mike Soltys and asked him about the risk of returning to the site of Florida State's 59-0 demolition of the Gamecocks a year earlier. That massacre was also beamed nationally by ESPN.

"We've still got people around here shaking their head over that Florida State game," Soltys said. "That was awful. We're just hoping for a good game."

The broadcast team of Ron Franklin and Kevin Kiley had to use their filler material early. Clemson quickly commenced a 45-0 destruction that remains the most thorough in the long history of the rivalry, aside from a 51-0 Clemson victory in 1900.

The Tigers were up 14-0 before the Gamecocks ran two offensive plays. They were up 24-0 at the half after Allen ran for ninety-seven yards and two touchdowns on fourteen carries before reinjuring his knee.

Wearing orange pants for the first time in an enemy stadium, Clemson ended the game with a 455-155 advantage in total yardage. During the fourth quarter, as South Carolina fans filed out of Williams-Brice Stadium, Clemson faithful taunted them by mimicking the Seminoles' famous Tomahawk Chop.

Sophomore fullbacks Tony Kennedy and Junior Hall had played sparingly to this point, but injuries to Allen and Wesley McFadden allowed them to join in the fun. They combined for ninety-eight rushing yards and had long touchdown runs as Clemson's offensive line abused the Gamecocks' defensive front.

Woods knew before the game that his team was vastly outmanned up front. In the post-game press conference, he was asked to identify the turning point.

"I think it was when we kicked off," he said. "It started right then."

Herman Helms of the *State* described the destruction in Sunday's paper: "Clemson is a Mike Tyson kind of football team which punishes its opponents. Big mooses on defense. Slashing runners on offense...A sellout crowd at the stadium and thousands of television viewers tuned into the ESPN network and were eye-witnesses to a slaughter. The USC athletic administration pushed hard to get the game on the tube. Are they sure they wanted to show this to the nation?"

Kirkland, then a sophomore linebacker, recalls now that everyone wanted to make the Gamecocks pay for what happened two years earlier in Columbia. The dominating win in 1988 wasn't enough.

> *We wanted to take it to them at their home. What happened in 1988 was satisfying, but it wasn't enough. Ever watch wrestling when the guy has the other guy down, has him beat and the ref is counting to three and the guy on top lets the other guy up right before he gets to three so he can beat him up some more? That was my personal feeling, and I think it was the team's feeling. And we got it all from the top. That's the way Danny Ford felt. He wanted to destroy them in Columbia. We wanted to shove it down their throats and teach them a lesson they'd never forget. And I don't think they ever did.*

Late in the game, Kiley marveled at what Ford had built.

"I don't think people around the country realize what a great coach Danny Ford is. Year in and year out, Clemson wins eight or nine games. They'll win nine games this year, and this was supposed to be a transition year because they lost thirty-seven players off last year's team. That's why a lot of people are picking them to win the national championship next year."

After going to the Florida Citrus Bowl in 1987 and 1988, Clemson was headed for the Gator Bowl to face West Virginia. The Mountaineers played Notre Dame for the national title the year before and were fueled by dynamic quarterback Major Harris, who finished third in the Heisman voting.

Ford had compiled a 5-0 record in Florida bowl games during his career, and a major part of his formula was arriving early and going through a rigorous pre-Christmas practice schedule that resembled summer two-a-days.

Clemson was a seven-point favorite, and players heard an overdose of Harris hype in the days leading up to the game. The Tigers also weren't in the best of moods after a flu bug swept through the team and caused twenty-three players to miss at least one practice session.

Ford spent the week denying reports from famous oddsmaker Danny Sheridan, who claimed on CNN that Ford would leave Clemson after the season.

Harris guided his offense ninety-six yards for a touchdown on the Mountaineers' first possession. But from there, Clemson's defense began to harass him at every turn. The Tigers were up just 10-7 early in the fourth quarter but poured it on for a 27-7 smashing that left everyone wondering how dominant this young team could be in 1990.

Clemson ran for 257 yards without Allen, who underwent knee surgery after the South Carolina game. Quarterback Chris Morocco was

Ford and West Virginia coach Don Nehlen before the 1989 Gator Bowl. The Mountaineers played for the national title the previous season. *Courtesy of Clemson University Sports Information Department.*

virtually flawless before suffering a concussion late, and his counterpart was bruised and battered by a relentless assault from the Tigers' defensive line and linebackers.

Kirkland terrorized the Mountaineers and earned MVP honors after totaling nine tackles, a forced fumble, a sack and three quarterback pressures.

In the run-up to the game, Harris had told reporters he was excited to face "new meat" in the Gator Bowl. Ford made a point to remind his players of the quote minutes before kickoff. On one of the many occasions Harris found himself on his back, linebacker Otis Moore stood over him.

"There's a lot more meat where that came from," Moore told him.

Harris lost three fumbles and was sacked twice. He finished with 119 yards passing and 17 rushing. He was nursing two sore elbows after the game, but he wasn't making any excuses.

"The elbows weren't a problem," he told reporters. "The only thing that was a problem was their defense...They smashed us."

Clemson's senior class became the first in ACC history to win thirty-eight games, and the first in school history to claim four consecutive bowl victories.

Ford was closing out a glorious decade in style with a third straight ten-win season. Since the inexplicable home loss to Georgia Tech in the seventh game, the Tigers had bulldozed their final five opponents by a combined score of 181-30.

It seemed fitting that the Gator Bowl played host to yet another instance of Ford knocking off a powerful program; that's where he beat Woody Hayes and Ohio State back in 1978 as a thirty-year-old in his first game as the Tigers' head coach.

Bill Curry was in trouble at Alabama, and some people speculated that Ford would leave for his alma mater. Veteran center Hank Phillips was asked about Ford's future after the game.

"Coach Ford isn't going anywhere," Phillips said in the *Independent-Mail*. "He can't afford to go anywhere. He's got it too good here. He told us flat-out he's not a quitter, and he's not quitting the team. He'll be here for the duration."

When Ford met with reporters the morning after the game, he'd slept only four hours after staying up late watching the replay of his team's win

Ford is carried to midfield by his players after the Tigers' 27-7 dismantling of West Virginia in the 1989 Gator Bowl. *Courtesy of Clemson University Sports Information Department.*

on ESPN. He was giddy about the victory and eager to talk about the promise of 1990 and beyond. Ford was forty-one years old and had the third-most wins of active coaches in Division I-A with a record of 96-29-4. The Tigers finished number eleven in the AP poll.

"If I don't make one mistake next year, it won't be that I get upset at what somebody says or what we should do," Ford said that day. "I'm not going to say our kids can't be good next year. I'm not going to say we don't deserve this or that. I'm not going to get into all that crap.

"We're going to mind our own business and we're going to try to be a football team that knows we're going to have pressure every week, have high expectations from everybody, and we're going to learn how to handle it. We're going to work on that in spring football. I don't think we do a good job of doing that. I think I know what to do."

Chapter 13

THE END

S everal days after the Tigers' mauling of West Virginia in the Gator
Bowl, the NCAA was back on the front pages of South Carolina
newspapers when it notified Clemson it was conducting an investigation
into specific charges of recruiting violations.

The NCAA alleged that a Clemson football coach, on two occasions in
the fall of 1985, used a player to distribute cash payments of $50 and $100
to "selected" players. The NCAA also claimed that a booster gave $50 to
two football players in 1984 and 1987. Another serious allegation: from
1984 to 1987, six coaches had made eleven illegal contacts to recruits.

All told, the NCAA said Clemson committed thirty-seven violations
of fourteen NCAA rules between 1984 and 1988. Clemson supporters
feared their football program would face stiff penalties after going
through probation from 1982 to 1984.

University president Max Lennon, who came to Clemson in 1986 after
a bitter power struggle between former president Bill Atchley and athletics
director Bill McLellan ultimately resulted in the ouster of both leaders,
expressed unequivocal cooperation with the NCAA in a prepared statement.

"The university and athletic department administrators are in full
agreement that the priority is protecting the integrity of the institution."

Nick Lomax, vice president of student affairs, reacted to the news by
telling reporters that the administration desired a football program "that
is beyond suspicion."

The End

"And another NCAA investigation is not being beyond suspicion," he said.

The NCAA scrutiny and rumors began in August 1989 after reports said that Clemson committed violations in its recruitment of heralded quarterback Michael Carr. On January 8, 1990, Carr told reporters he received a six-dollar hat during a visit to Clemson but was given nothing else during his recruitment.

Notre Dame quarterback Tony Rice made news when he told reporters that Clemson "wouldn't leave me alone" during his senior year at Woodruff High School. Rice signed with Notre Dame and led the Irish to a national title in 1988. "They didn't offer me any kind of money or anything," Rice said in an Associated Press story. "It was just the visits, my talking to them a lot—that broke the rule right there."

Danny Ford and athletics director Bobby Robinson met on January 11, but Robinson declined to comment on the discussion to reporters. Ford wasn't allowed to speak publicly on the NCAA investigation, and the lack of statements of support from his superiors fueled speculation that his future at Clemson was in doubt.

A number of recruits made official visits to Clemson on the weekend of January 12, and coaches told the recruits they weren't concerned that the NCAA investigation would result in major penalties. Quarterback Cale Gundy, a high school all-American from Oklahoma, said coaches told him the violations were "very little things, things that people shouldn't get upset about." The coaches told recruits that more than 90 percent of the thirty-seven alleged violations were not true. "They may get out of it," Gundy said in an AP article. "But if something happens, they think it'll be little."

The AP also quoted Malcolm Marshall, a running back recruit from North Carolina: "(Ford) said...the only way he'd get away from Clemson is if they fired him."

At 9:00 a.m. on Wednesday, January 17, Ford and Robinson met again in secrecy. A few hours later, lawyers from both sides were summoned to begin negotiating a settlement. Ford later said that he learned he was no longer the coach via a letter from Robinson—a letter Ford kept in his wallet for years. At about 10:00 p.m., Ford called his assistants off the recruiting trail and told them to return to Clemson.

There was no mention of these developments in Thursday's papers. At 8:00 a.m., Ford told his staff that he was resigning. By 10:00 a.m., Clemson's university switchboard was flooded with calls from fans wanting to know if the rumors were true. Callers were referred to another number that played a recording of a statement from Robinson announcing Ford's resignation.

Robinson told reporters the parting was the result of "basic philosophical differences" and "honest differences of opinion on certain aspects of the program." Ford met with his team at 11:30 a.m. and said he was resigning for the betterment of the university. In a release issued by the university, Ford denied any wrongdoing and said he was confident that he would be exonerated at the conclusion of the NCAA's investigation.

Ford went home to his farm for several hours in the afternoon and returned to campus at 3:30 p.m., driving a blue Ford pickup. He was accompanied by two friends carrying cardboard boxes as he made his way to his former office at the Jervey Athletic Center. Ford was greeted by a cluster of media. According to the *Greenville News*, he asked to read a reporter's copy of the university news release.

"Goddamn," he said, handing the release back to the reporter and walking inside.

In the immediate aftermath of Ford's resignation, the parting was viewed as a direct response to the NCAA's ongoing investigation. The front-page headline from the *State* the next day: "Ford ouster message to NCAA." On the *State*'s editorial page, cartoonist Robert Ariail scrawled an image of a Tiger wearing a Ford baseball cap. Accompanying the cartoon was a message: "**Fire Or Receive Death** penalty."

Embarrassing scandals and resulting probation had forced the departure of other high-profile coaches in recent years, including Barry Switzer at Oklahoma, Jackie Sherrill at Texas A&M and Galen Hall at Florida. SMU had resumed playing football after two years following a "death penalty" from the NCAA stemming from the discovery of rampant and systemic cheating. At N.C. State, basketball coach Jim Valvano would lose his job months later after the discovery of major violations. The NCAA also hammered Maryland and its basketball program after coach Bob Wade lied to investigators about providing money and clothing to recruits and players. An era of reform was at hand as the NCAA and college presidents tried to take greater responsibility for college athletics.

Ford received a settlement of more than $1 million from Clemson. He was due $190,000 annually over the next three years and received $100,000 to pay off the mortgage on his farm. Clemson gave him six season tickets to football games for the next three to five years.

The administration's refusal to specify the reasons for Ford's departure enraged fans. Robinson repeatedly stressed that the divorce was not related to the NCAA investigation. Some reports identified the real problem as Ford's power struggle with the administration. In the months preceding the 1989 season, Ford publicly criticized his superiors' opposition to a new dorm for athletes. Lennon and other administrators were moving forward with plans to build a new academic center for athletes instead, and Ford had openly encouraged boosters to make their voices heard.

The *Greenville News* quoted an unidentified source saying the rift over the dormitory "was the biggest thing between Danny Ford and the school."

"After they fought over that, it was never the same," the source told the newspaper.

Columnist Dan Foster summed up the tumultuous day this way:

> *Wearing the colors of a year-after-year national power made the Eighties a heady decade. And the continuing symbol of that was Ford. Somewhere during all that, though, those with responsibilities for the overall university became disenchanted with the image its football program gave it…Thousands are wondering if Clemson's teams will ever be as good again. All around, it was a very sad day.*

Venom flowed on radio talk shows as fans reacted to Ford's departure, which came less than three weeks after Clemson closed a 10-2 season with a Gator Bowl fleecing of West Virginia. The Tigers' roster in 1989 was full of young players, so national-title contention in coming years seemed realistic. The *State* conducted a phone poll asking readers if they agreed with the resignation, and those who did were outnumbered 703-199.

Players Ford left behind were in disbelief. They ripped the murky reasons given for his resignation and demanded his reinstatement. Stacy Fields, Vance Hammond and Scott Beville served as spokesmen for the team.

Garrison Hearst, a sought-after running back recruit from Lincolnton, Georgia, eliminated Clemson from his list of possible choices after hearing the news. He canceled plans for a January 20 visit to Clemson and ended up signing with Georgia.

Senator James Waddell, a trustee emeritus, told the *State* that he wasn't aware of Ford's resignation until Lennon called him the day the news broke. Five years earlier, as the board's chairman, Waddell played a large role in the ouster of Atchley after the president challenged McLellan.

"It used to be that we got involved in those things," Waddell told the newspaper. "But that's an administrative thing now, and that's the way it should be."

Lennon, who had pledged to restore the university's academic integrity when he took over four years earlier, told state lawmakers that the specifics behind Ford's departure should be kept secret and that an agreement had been made "that no further statement would be made by either party."

A day after his resignation was announced, Ford returned to the football offices and told reporters that he could not divulge details. He was asked

One of the last photos taken of Ford on a Clemson sideline. Nineteen days later, Ford was out as the Tigers' coach after eleven seasons. *Courtesy of Clemson University Sports Information Department.*

about criticism of the large settlement he received from the university. "I think it was fair," he told reporters. "I may never coach football again for the rest of my life. And I might have coached fifteen more years here."

On Friday night, a candlelight vigil attracted thousands to Bowman Field on Clemson's campus. The gathering quickly became edgy and turned into a protest as the masses moved to the lawn of the president's home. Much of the football team was present, and players were openly saying they planned to boycott the 1990 season if Ford or one of his assistants were not in charge.

A sign in the crowd read: "CU later MAX." Another read: "IPNAY: I'll Pay Nothing for a Year." One fan screamed: "Get out Max. That's our house." A state trooper told the *News and Courier*: "I haven't seen anything like this since the 60s."

The masses churning on Lennon's lawn had no idea he was in Memphis interviewing Arkansas coach Ken Hatfield. Arkansas had granted him permission to speak with Hatfield two days earlier, the day before Ford's resignation was announced. Robinson, Lennon and Lomax interviewed Hatfield at a Memphis hotel. Clemson initially reached out to Hatfield through Jack Crowe, a Razorbacks assistant who had served under Ford from 1986 to 1988.

On Saturday, Robinson spent several hours in Clemson conducting interviews with Ford assistants Chuck Reedy and Bill Oliver. That night, Ford received a rousing ovation when he showed up at Littlejohn Coliseum for Clemson's basketball game against Hofstra. Fans booed the presence of Lennon and Robinson.

Later that night, Robinson called Hatfield and offered him the job. Hatfield accepted, and by Sunday afternoon, he was in Clemson walking arm in arm with Clemson legend Frank Howard as they made their way to the introductory press conference at Memorial Stadium.

In six years at Arkansas, Hatfield had amassed a 55-17-1 record. He was coming off back-to-back 10-win seasons. He had won back-to-back Southwest Conference titles, and he'd built a squeaky-clean reputation in a scandal-ridden league. He even ran an option offense, a staple under Ford.

A segment of Clemson fans was still in a boiling rage just three days after Ford's resignation, and about two hundred of them showed outside the entrance to the Death Valley press box to blast Lennon and Robinson.

A sign read: "FIRE MAX & BOBBY; RE-HIRE DANNY." A portion of the crowd began a "We want Danny" chant. Howard, who a few days earlier said Clemson football would be "set back one hundred years" if it lost Ford, admonished the fans who weren't showing proper respect to Hatfield. "Don't make that feller feel bad," he told them.

After introducing Hatfield inside the press conference, Robinson quipped: "That's the first applause I've had in a while. It might be the last for a while, too." Lennon called this day the beginning of his "vision for our second century." He told the board of trustees that the forty-six-year-old Hatfield "represents all that intercollegiate athletics is supposed to be."

"That is, we are committed to Clemson to make sure that we are appropriately addressing our priorities, and that we, in fact, remember that 'student-athletes' has student first."

Hatfield addressed the crowd outside as he departed, saying the boos and barbs didn't bother him. "It shows you care. You care enough to show up and show support. There is too much apathy in the world. There is no apathy at Clemson University. You care. You hurt. And I hurt."

Robinson was under twenty-four-hour police protection after receiving threats in the wake of Thursday's news. SLED, campus police and city police provided the assistance.

Talk of a boycott dissipated after Hatfield met with players. Oliver, who served as a defensive assistant since 1986, left for a position at Alabama. Reedy, who was with Ford at Clemson from the beginning, ended up taking a job at Baylor as offensive coordinator. In an interview with the *Independent-Mail*, Oliver assessed the future of a program that had amassed a 38-8-2 record the previous four seasons.

"The only thing I know is coach Ford left that thing healthy, talent-wise. For the next three years they ought to be gangbusters. I wish all the players well. I do know the closeness that developed in the 1989 season, because the squad was so young...The sky can be the limit."

Three months later, Clemson went before the NCAA's Committee on Infractions in Kansas City. Ford and his lawyer were included in the ten-member entourage representing Clemson. Also present were Lennon, Robinson and Hatfield.

The End

Virginia faculty athletics representative Alan Williams was chairman of the Committee on Infractions, but he removed himself from the Clemson case to avoid a conflict of interest. In 1982, Williams was part of a group of ACC faculty athletics representatives who slapped Clemson with an extra year of probation beyond the NCAA's two-year punishment. Williams was present that day in Kansas City and told reporters that college presidents had "grabbed the bull by the horns" in an attempt to clean up college athletics.

The Clemson contingent spent four hours before the committee in Kansas City. Lennon emerged from the meeting and said he anticipated penalties from the NCAA while adding that he was "disturbed" to be in such a predicament.

"This is a very serious issue because the university is the place where we expect to find some integrity," he told reporters. "This is a very serious matter. It's regrettable that this kind of thing had to happen."

Ford went to Kansas City seeking to clear his name. He told reporters he was "very pleased" after the hearing. "What comes out in the committee's report is the most important thing," he said.

The NCAA's verdict came on May 31: one year of probation, but no scholarship reductions or bans on TV and bowl appearances. The NCAA said there was no pattern of cash payments, no lack of institutional control. The major violations were two instances of a booster giving two players small cash sums in 1985 and 1987. Clemson disassociated itself from the booster, and the NCAA determined the school had made ample efforts to educate its fans on the rules of recruiting.

Clemson supporters rejoiced after spending months fretting about long bans on bowl games and television appearances. Linebacker Levon Kirkland, who still had two years of college eligibility remaining, told reporters he "about jumped through the ceiling" after watching the NCAA's announcement on TV.

"The NCAA did show it has a heart," he said in the *Herald-Journal* of Spartanburg. "With all the teams that get lots of years of probation, you usually think that the NCAA doesn't have a heart. But I think that they listened to what the school had to say and just gave us a slap on the wrist."

While cautioning that another major violation within the next five years would subject Clemson to the two-year "death penalty," the NCAA commended the school for learning from its mistakes and instituting an effective compliance and monitoring system. The NCAA also vindicated Ford in its seven-page report, clearing him and his former staff of any sanctions. At a press conference with Robinson, NCAA director of enforcement Chuck Smrt said Ford's resignation didn't carry any influence on the severity of penalties.

Foster of the *Greenville News* wrote: "Only a dreamer could have entertained hopes for any better verdict than Clemson got Thursday from the NCAA Committee on Infractions."

Ken Burger of the *News and Courier*: "It was the day the Tigers stood squarely in front of the firing squad and got only a flesh wound. The question now is whether the guns were loaded."

The day after the NCAA released its findings, Ford held a press conference in Greenville. He'd lost almost twenty-five pounds working on his farm the previous four months. In an hour-long session with reporters, Ford said he might not have resigned had he known what the NCAA's verdict would be. He said he didn't believe he had a choice.

"It was a situation where a separation was wanted and it was done," he told the media that day. "I don't think I had the option of being the coach at Clemson…I think things happened rather quickly at that period of time. You know, when you play cards and you're in a poker game, you got to play what they've dealt to you and when it's your turn to play. If I had a chance to play the cards over, well, maybe that's a fair question for both people now. But it doesn't matter. The sixty-minute game is over. Who won? I don't know. Time will tell."

Ford was asked about his conflicts with Lennon over the athletics dorm and learning center. Less than a year later, NCAA presidents would vote to phase out athletics dorms on college campuses. "I guess he's a sincere president in what he's trying to get accomplished," Ford said. "I was sincere in what I was trying to get accomplished in our football program."

Ford responded to the speculation that Clemson pushed him out in exchange for lighter penalties from the NCAA. "At one time, I thought there might have been a deal working. But I don't believe that."

Ford said the oath of secrecy "is something the university wants to live with and something I want to live with."

"If I want to get back in coaching, I'm going to need all the help I can get. So I'm not going to sit here and throw darts at anybody. And I don't think they'll throw darts at me."

Ford said his football program had become "as clean as any of them," and he seemed irritated that the administration didn't give him or his staff any credit for the improvements cited by the NCAA. "Institutional control is not just the administration," he said. "I think our checks and balances as a coaching staff was super. The biggest improvement that the NCAA saw in our program from 1982 to now is what the coaches were doing."

Ford was asked if he'd received any calls from other schools looking for a coach. "If I did, I would call that coach and tell him 'You've got a low-life son of a gun for a president,'" he said, drawing a burst of laughter from the press. "Don't take that wrong," he said. "I like Dr. Lennon."

Ford told the reporters he was now back on the coaching market. A few fans managed to work their way into the press conference, and one of them asked the coach if he'd consider returning to Clemson under a different administration.

The response: "My era is over."

APPENDIX

Danny Ford's Year-by-Year Records

1978: 1-0
1979: 8-4, 4-2 ACC
1980: 6-5, 2-4 ACC
1981: 12-0, 6-0 ACC (conference champs, national champs)
1982: 9-1-1, 6-0 ACC (conference champs)
1983: 9-1-1, 7-0 ACC
1984: 7-4, 5-2 ACC
1985: 6-6, 4-3 ACC
1986: 8-2-2, 5-1-1 ACC (conference champs)
1987: 10-2, 6-1 ACC (conference champs)
1988: 10-2, 6-1 ACC (conference champs)
1989: 10-2, 5-2 ACC

FORD'S BOWL RESULTS:

1978: Gator Bowl, Ohio State, 17-15 W
1979: Peach Bowl, Baylor, 24-18 L
1981: Orange Bowl, Nebraska, 22-15 W
1985: Independence Bowl, Minnesota, 20-13 L
1986: Gator Bowl, Stanford, 27-21 W
1987: Citrus Bowl, Penn State, 35-10 W

1988: Citrus Bowl, Oklahoma, 13-6 W
1989: Gator Bowl, West Virginia, 27-7 W

CLEMSON'S FINAL RANKING IN THE ASSOCIATED PRESS POLL DURING FORD'S TENURE:

1978: 6
1981: 1
1982: 8
1983: 11
1986: 17
1987: 12
1988: 9
1989: 12

WINNING PERCENTAGE BY ACC COACHES IN OVERALL GAMES:

1. Frank Beamer, Virginia Tech: 84-24-0 (.777)
2. Bobby Bowden, Florida State: 173-53-1 (.764)
3. Danny Ford, Clemson: 96-29-4 (.760)
4. Lou Holtz, N.C. State: 33-12-3 (.719)
5. Ken Hatfield, Clemson: 32-13-1 (.707)
6. Jim Tatum, Maryland and North Carolina: 41-19-2 (.677)
7. Jerry Claiborne, Maryland: 72-37-3 (.656)
8. Paul Johnson, Georgia Tech: 34-19-0 (.641)
9. Dick Sheridan, N.C. State: 52-29-3 (.637)
10. Dick Crum, North Carolina: 72-41-3 (.634)
(three seasons minimum)

ABOUT THE AUTHOR

Larry Williams has covered Clemson football on a daily basis since early 2004, when he joined the *Post and Courier* of Charleston, South Carolina. In 2008, he moved to Tigerillustrated.com, the most popular subscription-based Clemson site on the Internet. From 1999 to 2003, he worked as a sportswriter at the *Augusta Chronicle* in Georgia and covered college sports at Clemson, South Carolina and Georgia. He also covered the Super Bowl, the Final Four and the Masters. In 2007, he was named South Carolina Sportswriter of the Year by the National Sportscasters and Sportswriters Association. In 2011, he and Travis Haney co-authored the book *Classic Clashes of the Carolina-Clemson Football Rivalry: A State of Disunion.* He lives in the Clemson area with his wife and two daughters.

Visit us at
www.historypress.net